Heinemann **Scottish** History
for Standard Grade

Elizabeth Trueland

Series editor: Jim McGonigle

International Cooperation
AND
Conflict
1890s–1920s

www.heinemann.co.uk

✓ Free online support
✓ Useful weblinks
✓ 24 hour online ordering

01865 888058

Inspiring generations

Heinemann is an imprint of Pearson Education Limited, a company incorporated in England and Wales, having its registered office at Edinburgh Gate, Harlow, Essex, CM20 2JE. Registered company number: 872828

Heinemann is a registered trademark of Pearson Education Limited

First published 2004

09

10 9 8 7 6

British Library Cataloguing in Publication Data is available from the British Library on request.

ISBN 978 0 435326 90 6

Designed by Hicksdesign

Produced by Kamae Design, Oxford

Original illustrations © Harcourt Education Limited, 2003

Illustrated by Jeff Edwards

Printed and bound in China (CTPS/06)

Cover photo: Scottish soldiers returning from combat July 1916, by Francois Fleming © Mary Evans picture library

Picture research by Charlotte Lippmann

Acknowledgements

The publishers would like to thank the following for permission to use photographs:

AKG p.20; p. 31; Associated Press p.5; The British Library p.75, p.92; Corbis p.72; Corbis/Michael St.Mair Sheil p.4 (right); DHM Berlin p.78, p.80; Getty Images p.60; p.61; p.84; Imperial War Museum p.4 (left); p.33, p.39; p.43; p.49; p.52; p.53; p.67; p.69; p.73; p.79; p.81; Mary Evans Picture Library p.8; p.12; p.24; p.45; National Army Museum p.38; Punch p.9 (left); p.17; p.21; p.27; p.66; p.91; Robert Hunt Library p.13; Sotheby's p.50; Source Unknown p.9 (right); p.34, p.47; p.74; Wellcome Library p.41.

Every effort has been made to contact copyright holders of material reproduced in this book. Any omissions will be rectified in subsequent printings if notice is given to the publishers.

Written source acknowledgements

The author and publisher gratefully acknowledge the following publications from which written sources in the book are drawn. In some sentences the wording or sentence structure has been simplified:

8B	A.J.P. Taylor, *The Course of German History* (Routledge, 1988)
25B	Ruth Henig, *The Origins of the First World War* (Routledge, 2002)
33D	A.J.P. Taylor, *The First World War* (London, 1963)
33E	Niall Ferguson, *The Pity of War* (Allen Lane, 1998)
34K	Gerald De Groot, *Blighty: British society in the era of the Great War* (Longman, 1996)
38B	George Coppard, *With a machine gun to Cambrai* (Cassell, 1999)
40E	George Coppard, *With a machine gun to Cambrai* (Cassell, 1999)
41I	Malcolm Brown, *The Imperial War Museum Book of the First World War* (Sidgwick and Jackson, 1991)
41K	George Coppard, *With a machine gun to Cambrai* (Cassell, 1999)
46E	George Coppard, *With a machine gun to Cambrai* (Cassell, 1999)
46H	Duff Cooper, *Haig* (Doubleday, 1936)
47K	Robin Prior and Trevor Wilson in 'The First World War', *History Today* magazine (1991)
50C	Lyn MacDonald, *1914–18: Voices and Images of the Great War* (Penguin, 1991)
52J	Peter Simkins, *The First World War: The Western Front, 1914–16* (Osprey, 2000)
51H	Vera Brittain, *Chronicle of Youth: Great War Diary, 1913–17*, ed. Alan Bishop (Phoenix, 2000)
53L	George Coppard, *With a machine gun to Cambrai* (Cassell, 1999)
54M	John Terraine, *White Heat: the new warfare 1914–18* (Sidgwick and Jackson, 1982)
57C	Robin Prior and Trevor Wilson in 'The First World War', *History Today* magazine (1991)
61G	Jay Winter & Blaine Baggett, *1914 – 18: the Great War and the shaping of the twentieth century* (BBC Books, 1996)
61H	ed. Hew Strachan, *The Oxford Illustrated History of the First World War* (Oxford University Press, 1998)
66A	Gerard De Groot, *Blighty: British society in the era of the Great War* (Longman, 1996)
66B	The Times, (editorial) 14 May 1915
68G	Gerard De Groot, *Blighty: British society in the era of the Great War* (Longman, 1996)
69H	Gerard De Groot, *Blighty: British society in the era of the Great War* (Longman, 1996)
73D	The *Observer newspaper*, October 1917
74E	Vera Brittain, *Chronicle of Youth: Great War Diary, 1913–17*, ed. Alan Bishop (Phoenix, 2000)
76H	Arthur Marwick, *The Deluge: British society and the First World War* (Macmillan, 1991)
77I	Gerard De Groot, *Blighty: British society in the era of the Great War* (Longman, 1996)
82H	A.J.P. Taylor, *The First World War* (London, 1963)

CONTENTS

INTRODUCTION
International Cooperation and Conflict

What's it all about?

In this book you will learn about:

- why war broke out in 1914
- the impact of the war on both soldiers and civilians
- how new technology affected the way soldiers fought the war
- the work of the peacemakers at the end of the war
- the attempts to prevent another major war after 1919.

THE DEATH OF A BRITISH SOLDIER

Source A

A letter informing a family of the death of a British soldier during the First World War.

When the guns stopped firing at the eleventh hour of the eleventh day of the eleventh month, 1918, the First World War, or Great War, came to an end after more than four years of fighting. No one knows how many people died during the four years of fighting but it is estimated that over 9.5 million soldiers died and a further 15 million were seriously injured.

It is hard to understand what this number of casualties means in terms of human suffering and misery. When we read that 20,000 British soldiers died on the first day of the attack on the Somme, 1 July 1916, it is difficult to imagine the scale of the slaughter. It is not surprising that almost as soon as the fighting had stopped, people began to question how such a terrible war had come about in the first place.

Source B

Some of the 12,000 graves at Tyne Cot cemetery in Belgium. Although Tyne Cot is the largest of the First World War cemeteries on the Western Front, similar graves can be found throughout Belgium and northern France. Many of the British graves are unnamed, stating instead 'Known only to God' because it was not possible to identify the shattered remains of the soldier buried there.

WHAT CAUSES WARS?

One historian has counted over 300 separate wars in the 60 years since the end of the Second World War. You may know of parts of the world where people are currently at war.

Source C

Soldier fighting in Iraq, 2003.

⋯∴ Activity

1 Why do countries, or groups of people within countries, fight each other?

    Working in groups of three or four, see how many reasons you can identify. You should appoint one member of the group to keep a note of your ideas.

2 Compare your answers with those of the other groups in the class.

3 Now use all of the ideas produced during your brainstorming session to complete this mind map. You can add as much as you want to this basic diagram.

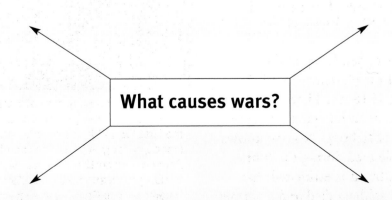

What causes wars?

RIVALRY BETWEEN THE GREAT POWERS

What were the tensions in Europe before 1914?

What's it all about?

Between 1890 and 1914 there were rising tensions between the most powerful European countries. Each of the major powers tended to regard the others as rivals. These tensions led to increased competition between the countries.

THE GREAT POWERS OF EUROPE

There were two **World Wars** during the twentieth century. In both wars the most powerful countries in the world at that time, the 'Great Powers', were fighting each other to defend what they claimed as their interests. Because the First World War started in Europe, historians consider the rivalry and tensions between the Great Powers of Europe in the years before 1914 to have caused the war.

Glossary

World War: a war involving a large number of different countries in many parts of the world.

The Great Powers of Europe in 1914.

The overseas Empires of the Great Powers.

1 The two maps and the barchart on page 6 provide information about different aspects of national power. Explain why each aspect is important when assessing how powerful a nation is.

2 Using the information provided, which European nation do you think was the most powerful in 1914? Is it difficult to reach a decision – and if so, why?

3 What conclusion can you reach about possible causes of conflict and rivalry between the Great Powers of Europe in the years immediately before 1914?

THE GROWTH OF GERMANY

The map on page 6 shows Europe in 1914. Sixty years earlier, the map of Europe had looked very different – the German Empire did not exist. Instead, there were a number of small German states, of which the largest and most important was Prussia. The map below shows that in 1848 even Prussia's lands were divided. After 1850, many people looked to Prussia to unite all of the German-speaking people outside the Austro–Hungarian Empire into one country.

Between 1862 and 1870, the King of Prussia and his Chancellor, Otto von Bismarck, managed to unify Germany. Twice Prussia went to war with neighbouring countries to make sure that it emerged as the leader of a united Germany. Then, in 1870, Prussia fought France. The Franco-Prussian War of 1870–1 resulted in a humiliating defeat for the French. At the end of the war, Germany demanded that the French should pay a very large **indemnity**. To make matters worse, the French had to **cede** most of Alsace and Lorraine to Germany. These areas had been part of France for more than 200 years and Lorraine, in particular, was rich in coal and iron ore. Losing Alsace and Lorraine was a bitter blow to the French.

Glossary

indemnity: a sum of money which had to be paid as compensation.

cede: to give away.

To humiliate the French further, the new German Empire was proclaimed at a ceremony on 18 January 1871 in the Hall of Mirrors at the Palace of Versailles, just outside Paris. The Prussian ruler now took the title of Kaiser, or Emperor, of Germany.

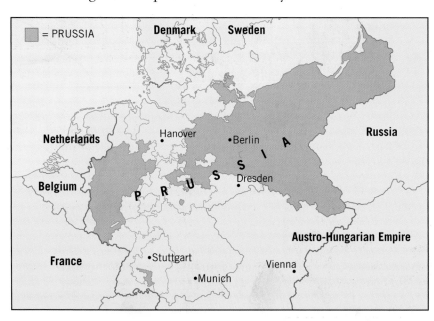

Prussia in 1848.

The impact on Britain and France

The growth of Germany affected relations between the Great Powers. After 1871, French governments planned for the day when they would be able to avenge their humiliating defeat and the loss of Alsace and Lorraine. They increased the size of the French army and built massive forts on the border between France and Germany.

GERMANISATION, par BROUSSET

— Je n'en veux pas! Je n'en veux pas!

A French illustration (1911) reflecting resentment in Alsace and Lorraine at the attempts to make them part of Germany. The German bully is forcing a military helmet onto the little French boy's head while the boy cries 'I don't want it'. The children's clothes make it clear they live in Alsace and Lorraine.

After 1871, the German economy grew faster than that of Britain. As a result, many people in Britain viewed Germany as an economic rival.

In 1888, Kaiser Wilhelm I died. His son and heir, Frederick, was dying of cancer and a few months later Wilhelm's 29-year-old grandson was crowned Wilhelm II. The new Kaiser was eager to prove that the German Empire was the most powerful country in Europe. However, his arrogance upset the governments of many of the other European countries.

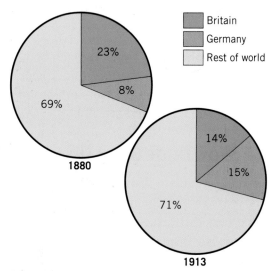

Britain

Germany

Rest of world

1880

23%

8%

69%

1913

14%

15%

71%

British and German production of manufactured goods, 1880–1913, shown as a percentage of the world total.

Source B

Within a few years, Prussia had risen from being the weakest and least regarded of the Great Powers to become the dominant state of the European continent.

A.J.P. Taylor, writing in 1945.

1   Describe the growth of Germany between 1848 and 1890. Use the text and Source B to answer this question.

2   Explain why relations between the Great Powers of Europe changed between 1848 and 1890. Use the information in the maps, pie charts and sources, as well as the text, to answer this question.

⋯⋗ *Activity*

Historians disagree about the part Kaiser Wilhelm II played in the events leading to the outbreak of war in 1914.

Was the Kaiser really a threat to European stability? Use the school library or the Internet to research this issue.

You should consider:

- the Kaiser's childhood and education
- his relationship to the British and Russian royal families
- his actions and behaviour as Kaiser of Germany.

You should be prepared to present your conclusions to the rest of the class.

... IN CONCLUSION

⋯⋗ ■   By 1914 there was rivalry between the main European countries, and this rivalry created tensions.

- ■ The growth of the German Empire made tensions in Europe worse.
- ■ The French were determined to regain Alsace and Lorraine.

PRACTISE YOUR ENQUIRY SKILLS

Source C

L'ENFANT TERRIBLE!

A *Punch* cartoon of 1890, 'L' Enfant Terrible!' (the badly behaved child). The man standing up is the Kaiser.

Source D

HE WONT BE HAPPY TILL HE GETS IT

A British cartoon from 1914.

1   Discuss the point of view of the artist who drew Source A (page 8). What message did he want to convey?

2   How useful are Sources C and D as evidence of attitudes towards Germany between 1890 and 1914?

2 TENSIONS IN THE BALKANS

What was the significance of the Balkans before 1914?

What's it all about?

There were problems in **the Balkans** as the Turkish Empire lost control over the region. Austria-Hungary and Russia were also affected by the changes that were taking place in south-eastern Europe.

THE DECLINE OF THE TURKISH EMPIRE

In 1850, the Turkish Empire extended into much of the Balkans, in south-eastern Europe. Many different groups of people, each with their own customs, language and identity, lived under Turkish rule and longed to be independent.

The Greeks won their independence from the Turkish Empire in the 1820s. Then, in 1878, Rumania, Serbia, Bulgaria and Montenegro were granted independence because the Turks could no longer maintain control in the region. By 1900, a much smaller area of the European mainland remained under Turkish control.

The Balkans and the Austro-Hungarian Empire in 1900.

Glossary

the Balkans: an area in south-east Europe which had been part of the Turkish Empire for hundreds of years.

Slavs: a large group of people living in eastern Europe.

Although most of the people who lived in these newly independent countries were **Slavs**, they competed with each other from the start. This rivalry was often based on mistrust and hatred that went back hundreds of years. As a result, independence for these countries did not end the problems in the area.

As the Turkish Empire became weaker, the other European powers looked to advance their own interests in the region.

Russia's interest in the Balkans

A new movement known as Pan-Slavism developed in Russia, the most powerful of the Slav nations. Pan-Slavism aimed to bring about a federation of Slavs under Russian leadership. Many people within Russia saw this as a way of increasing Russian influence in the area, and so encouraged the new, independent states in the Balkans to look to Russia for support.

Austria-Hungary's interest in the Balkans

Austria-Hungary viewed Pan-Slavism and Russia's growing influence in the Balkans with alarm. Russia and Austria-Hungary had been rivals in the region for a long time and now the situation was becoming extremely tense.

Like the Turkish Empire, the Austro-Hungarian Empire was vast and ruled over people of many different nationalities who wanted to be independent, including Slavs. Fearing that independence for one group of people would undermine the whole of the **multinational** Empire, Austria-Hungary was determined to retain control over her lands in the Balkans and, if necessary, to extend them. This situation threatened to bring Austria-Hungary into conflict with Russia.

Glossary

multinational: containing people of many different nationalities.

The Serbian challenge

Serbia was the most powerful of the new Balkan states. Although Serbia had gained its independence in 1878, the Serbs remained dissatisfied. In particular, they resented the fact that there were many Serbs living in neighbouring Bosnia, an area that the Austrian army had occupied since 1875. Austria-Hungary was determined that Serbia should not acquire Bosnia, as a larger Serbia would threaten Austrian ambitions in the area.

1 Describe the main changes in the Balkans between 1870 and 1900.

2 'By 1900, there was a real danger that the problems in the Balkans could lead to war.'

Explain why there was a danger of war in the Balkans by the beginning of the twentieth century.

In your answer you should should refer to:

■ the decline of the Turkish Empire

■ the conflicting interests of Austria-Hungary and Russia in the region

■ the ambitions of the new, independent Balkan states, including Serbia.

... IN CONCLUSION

- ■ The Turkish Empire was losing control over its lands in Europe.
- ■ Russia hoped to benefit from the decline of the Turkish Empire by befriending the new Balkan states.
- ■ Pan-Slavism encouraged the people of south-east Europe to look to Russia for leadership.
- ■ Austria-Hungary was worried about changes in the Balkans.
- ■ The Austro-Hungarian Empire included many Slavs who were demanding independence.

3 BUILDING EMPIRES

How did the race for land overseas affect the Great Powers?

What's it all about?

The overseas empires of European countries were another cause of tension. Imperial rivalry increased hostility between the nations of Europe.

EUROPEAN RIVALRIES ABROAD

You have already learned from the map on page 6 that several European countries ruled over large overseas empires by the end of the nineteenth century. In addition, these European countries influenced or controlled other less developed countries in Africa and Asia. Britain had by far the largest empire but France, too, had many overseas **colonies**, particularly in South-East Asia and Africa.

Glossary

colonies: areas of land overseas that belong to an Empire.

imperialism: extending a nation's power or influence over other countries.

Colonies were important for a number of reasons:

- They were an important source of raw materials and food.
- They provided soldiers during war.
- They were an important market for investment and manufactured goods.
- The location of some overseas colonies was strategically important, allowing European countries to protect their interests in other countries abroad.

Britain and France fall out over the Sudan

Imperialism added to the rivalry between the Great Powers at the end of the nineteenth century. War between Britain and France was a real possibility in 1898 when French and British armies both claimed the village of Fashoda in the southern Sudan. Although a remote area on the upper Nile, Fashoda was strategically important to both countries. The French planned to link their African colonies from west to east, while the British hoped to build a railway from Cairo in the north to the Cape, the southern tip of Africa. Eventually, the French government ordered their troops to withdraw, but only after several weeks of high tension.

Source A

A French cartoon from 1898 showing France as Little Red Riding Hood and Britain as the Big Bad Wolf.

Germany demands 'a place in the sun' ...

In the meantime, Germany wanted to be involved in the 'scramble' for land in Africa. In 1897, the German Chancellor stated, 'We too demand a place in the sun.' During the 1890s, Britain was prepared to support Germany's desire to acquire colonies in Africa and there was even talk of an alliance between Britain and Germany. However, when Britain went to war with the **Boer** republics in southern Africa in 1899, Germany sold weapons to the Boers. The Boer War (1899–1902) proved a difficult and expensive war for the British, and highlighted the costs of maintaining and defending its empire.

Glossary

Boer: A Dutch settler in Africa.

armaments: a country's military strength.

After 1902, the British government was determined to avoid expensive colonial wars. In particular, they wanted to avoid a colonial war with France. Therefore, in 1904, Britain and France settled their colonial differences and signed a 'friendly understanding' (see Chapter 4). From then on, Britain supported French rather than German imperial interests.

DID IMPERIALISM LEAD TO WAR?

By 1918, many people believed imperialism had caused the First World War. In the years before 1914, European businesses were looking for new markets abroad and this led to demands for more territory, which increased rivalry between the Great Powers. As tensions increased, so did spending on **armaments**.

However, most historians today reject this view. Although it looked as if Britain might declare war on Russia in the 1880s and on France in the 1890s, these wars never happened. After 1900, Britain, France and Russia began to settle their imperial differences.

When the European powers went to war in 1914, imperialism was one cause of tension that made the countries suspicious of each other. However, there were other, more important reasons for the outbreak of war.

Source B

An Italian cartoon from 1915.

L'INGORDO
TROP DUR

1 Why did European countries want to acquire colonies outside Europe?

2 Describe one occasion when imperial rivalry nearly led to war between two European powers.

3 How important was imperialism as a cause of the First World War?

... IN CONCLUSION

- ■ European countries competed with each other to expand their overseas empires.
- ■ Imperialism increased tensions between European countries before 1914.
- ■ Some historians have claimed that imperialism was responsible for the outbreak of the First World War.

PRACTISE YOUR ENQUIRY SKILLS

1   How useful is Source A (page 12) as evidence of imperial rivalry in the 1890s?

2   What does Source B (page 13) suggest about the causes of the First World War?

4 THE TRIPLE ALLIANCE VERSUS THE TRIPLE ENTENTE

How did the alliances bring about war in 1914?

What's it all about?

By 1914, Europe was divided into two rival systems – the Triple Alliance and the Triple Entente. The existence of these rival 'armed camps' may have increased the likelihood of a major war.

THE TWO 'ARMED CAMPS'

In the years before the First World War, Europe was divided into two rival groups of states – the Triple **Alliance**, which consisted of Germany, Austria-Hungary and Italy, and the Triple **Entente**, consisting of France, Russia and Britain. Because each of these countries was also involved in an **arms race** by 1914, Europe became increasingly divided into two hostile 'armed camps'. Some historians believe that the existence of the Triple Alliance and the Triple Entente made it more likely that any European war which involved one of these countries, would lead to war between all of the Great Powers.

Glossary

alliance: a definite commitment made by two or more countries to provide military support for fellow members of the alliance in certain circumstances.

entente: an understanding between two or more countries in which no definite commitments are made.

arms race: when countries compete against each other to have the greatest military and weapons strength.

THE TRIPLE ALLIANCE ...

Bismarck's ambitions

After the unification of Germany in 1871, the German Chancellor Bismarck had three main aims. These were:

- to keep France isolated from possible allies so that she would find it difficult to plan a war of revenge to win back Alsace and Lorraine
- to remain on good terms with Russia to prevent the possibility of a future alliance between France and Russia
- to persuade Austria-Hungary to enter into an alliance with Germany.

Bismarck maintained friendly relations with Russia through the Three Emperors' League, an informal agreement between Germany, Austria-Hungary and Russia. In 1879, Germany and Austria-Hungary signed the secret Dual Alliance, agreeing to support each other in the event of an attack by Russia or France. Three years later, in 1882, Italy joined the Alliance and it became known as the Triple Alliance.

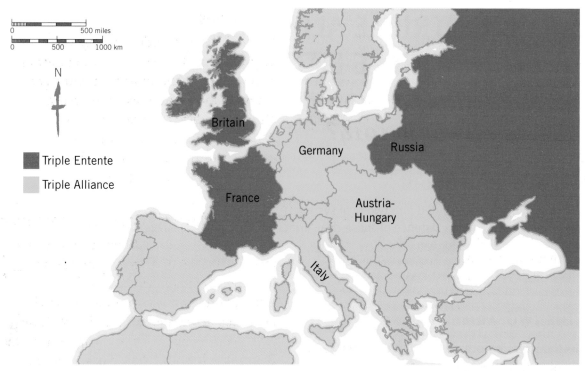

The Triple Alliance and the Triple Entente. Italy did not support Germany and Austria in 1914. In fact, when war started she began negotiations with Britain and France and entered the war on the side of the Entente in 1915.

Until the mid 1880s it seemed that Bismarck had succeeded in keeping France isolated from Russia. However, the Three Emperors' League was proving increasingly difficult to maintain because Russia and Austria-Hungary had conflicting interests in the Balkans, and it finally dissolved in 1887. Germany then signed a treaty with Russia in 1887, but this too was dropped in 1890 when Bismarck was forced to resign. This meant that after 1890 Russia was free of any kind of commitment to Germany, at a time when France was looking for an ally.

... AND THE TRIPLE ENTENTE

France and Russia

During the winter of 1893–4, France and Russia signed the Franco-Russian Alliance. Bismarck's fears had now come true: Germany was encircled to the west and east by an alliance of two hostile countries.

British foreign policy

Until the late 1890s, Britain made no effort to enter into an alliance or treaty with other European powers. Instead, Britain remained in 'splendid isolation', believing that its empire and navy offered sufficient protection against invasion. However, by the end of the 1890s, Britain began to consider an alliance. At first, it looked as if an agreement might be made with Germany, but then in 1902 Britain signed an agreement with Japan – the Anglo-Japanese Alliance. The treaty was made because both countries feared Russian ambitions in the Far East.

Britain and France

The Boer War in Africa (1899–1902) had increased British awareness of the cost of defending its empire. Anxious to avoid further colonial conflict, Britain determined to resolve its differences with France. In 1904, talks began between the two countries, leading to the signing of the Entente Cordiale, or 'friendly understanding'. Although both countries agreed to settle their main imperial disputes, this was not a formal alliance because neither country committed itself to support the other during war.

The Entente Cordiale brought Britain and France steadily closer together and there was no further talk of an alliance between Britain and Germany.

Britain and Russia

In 1907, Britain settled its imperial disputes with Russia and both countries signed the Anglo-Russian Entente. The Triple Entente was now in existence, although it differed from the Triple Alliance because Britain was not committed to supporting her Entente partners in the event of a war.

France and Britain draw closer together

After 1904, Britain and France drew closer together. French and British generals began discussing military plans based on the assumption that the two countries would fight together in a future war. In 1912, the two countries reached a naval agreement: the British would patrol the Channel and the North Sea, and the French would patrol the Mediterranean. This meant that if Germany attacked France, Britain's navy would provide support in the Channel and the North Sea.

Although Britain had no definite commitment to support France if attacked, it was now more likely that Britain would become involved in any future war.

Source A

WHY NOT?
FRANCE (to RUSSIA). "AREN'T YOU GOING TO DANCE WITH MR. BULL?"
RUSSIA. "I THINK I SHOULD RATHER LIKE TO, IF HE WOULDN'T TREAD ON MY TOES."
FRANCE. "OH, BUT HE WON'T. HE'S IMPROVED IMMENSELY. I FIND HIM ADORABLE!"

A *Punch* cartoon about the Entente Cordiale, October 1905.

Source B

A policy aimed at the encirclement of Germany and seeking to form a ring of powers in order to isolate and paralyse it would be disastrous to the peace of Europe. The formation of such a ring around Germany would not be possible without exerting some pressure. Pressure gives rise to counter-pressure. And out of this pressure and counter-pressure finally explosions may arise.

Prince Bernhard von Bülow, Chancellor of Germany 1900–1909.

⋯⋮ *Activity*

1   Copy and complete the table below, writing in the countries that belonged to each group.

Three Emperors' League	
Dual Alliance	
Entente Cordiale	
Triple Alliance	
Triple Entente	

2   Write a paragraph explaining why the existence of the Triple Alliance and the Triple Entente made it more likely that war would involve all the major European powers.

... IN CONCLUSION

⋯⋮ ■ By 1914, Europe was divided into two 'armed camps': Germany, Austria-Hungary and Italy formed the Triple Alliance; the Triple Entente consisted of France, Russia and Britain.

PRACTISE YOUR ENQUIRY SKILLS

1   Look at Source A (page 17).

a) Why are France and Russia seated together?

b) Why was there a danger that Mr Bull might tread on Russia's toes?

c) What is the significance of Mr Bull's partner?

2   How useful is Source A as evidence of relations between the European powers in the early twentieth century? Give reasons for your answer.

3   Read Source B (page 17) carefully.

What was von Bülow's attitude towards the Triple Entente? Explain your answer with reference to the source.

5 THE ARMS RACE: PREPARATIONS FOR WAR?

Why was there an arms race?

What's it all about?

As tensions between the European powers rose, each country increased spending on its armed forces. France, Germany and Russia invested enormous sums of money in their armies, while Britain relied on the strength of its navy. When Germany started to build a modern navy, Britain became very alarmed.

THE IMPORTANCE OF A LARGE AND POWERFUL ARMY

As rivalry between the Great Powers increased, each country became more aware of the importance of its armed forces. Conflicts in the late nineteenth century, such as the American Civil War (1861–5) and the Franco-Prussian War (1870–1), had demonstrated the impact of new technology on traditional methods of fighting. They had also shown how swiftly a well-equipped army could defeat a major power. Thus, as international tensions increased, almost every European country spent more on defence. No country could risk being left behind in what had become an 'arms race'.

- After 1871, French governments planned for a war of revenge to win back Alsace and Lorraine.

- Both France and Germany developed huge **conscript** armies. This meant that all young men had to undergo a period of military training, after which they would enter the 'reserves' of men who could be called upon to fight.

- Railways were extended to make it easier to transport whole armies, and military timetables were drawn up so that troops and equipment could be moved efficiently.

- As weapons technology became more sophisticated, governments demanded the latest military equipment and armaments manufacturers grew wealthy.

Glossary

conscript: a person who has been compulsorily registered in the army.

REFORM OF THE BRITISH ARMY

Although there were relatively few full-time soldiers in Britain, a Scot, R. B. Haldane, reformed the army when he was appointed Secretary of State for War in 1905. Haldane created the General Staff to facilitate military planning and the British Expeditionary Force (BEF), which would be ready to send troops immediately to any trouble spots. Haldane also set up the Territorial Army, to provide back-up for the professional army, and the Officer Training Corps in schools and universities.

Source A

The Krupp armaments factory in Germany, 1909, where industrial methods were applied to weapons production.

---

1 Describe the ways in which France and Germany strengthened their armies.

2 The Krupp family, who owned the factory shown in Source A, provided the money for the German Naval League, an organisation that campaigned in favour of naval spending. Why do you think the Krupp family did this?

THE NAVAL RACE BETWEEN BRITAIN AND GERMANY

'Britannia rules the waves'

During the nineteenth century, Britain was the world's greatest sea power. The Royal Navy played a vital part in protecting Britain from the threat of invasion, and in safeguarding both its empire and overseas trade. The existence of Britain's navy justified the policy of 'splendid isolation' by which Britain did not enter into any formal alliances with other countries.

In 1889, Britain adopted the 'two-power standard'. This stated that the British navy must be larger than the fleets of the next two largest navies combined. In 1889, it was assumed that the next two largest navies were those of France and Russia. To ensure that Britain had a navy sufficiently powerful to meet the two-power standard, money was allocated to build eight first-class battleships.

Germany builds a fleet

Britain did not consider the German navy to be a threat until Kaiser Wilhelm II decided that Germany must have a modern fleet. The Kaiser believed that a fleet would establish Germany's position as a Great Power with interests overseas. In 1895, the Kiel Canal was opened, giving German ships easier access between the Baltic and the North Sea. Three years later the **Reichstag** passed the German Naval Law, and Germany began a major ship building programme.

Glossary

Reichstag: the German parliament.

In Britain, this was seen as a direct challenge. Popular stories in Britain at the time reflected increased suspicions about German naval ambitions, and many people demanded that Britain should increase its spending on the navy. A bestselling novel, *The Riddle of the Sands* (1903), described the discovery of a German plan to invade Britain using the fleet to transport thousands of troops across the North Sea. In 1906 the *Daily Mail* serialised another tale of a large-scale German invasion.

HMS Dreadnought

In 1904, Admiral Sir John Fisher was appointed First Sea Lord and he immediately set about modernising the navy. Older warships were scrapped and a new battleship was commissioned – *HMS Dreadnought*. This was the first of a revolutionary new type of battleship whose speed, armour plating and revolving gun turrets made all other battleships obsolete. *HMS Dreadnought* was successfully launched in February 1906.

The race to build the most new battleships

The launch of the *Dreadnought* created a new problem – since the rest of Britain's battleships were now out of date, what would happen if another country started to build battleships as technologically advanced as the *Dreadnought*?

When Germany launched a similarly modern type of battleship, the *Nassau*, in 1908, a naval race was underway. Both countries spent huge sums of money on ship building programmes. Germany announced plans to build twelve more *Nassau*-class ships over the next four years, causing widespread panic in Britain. Britain responded by building eight new *Dreadnoughts* in 1909. Germany's decision to widen the Kiel Canal, so that its largest battleships could quickly reach the North Sea, also threatened Britain's interests.

The naval race continued until the outbreak of the First World War in August 1914. By this time, Britain had launched 22 modern *Dreadnought*-class battleships and Germany had launched fifteen *Nassau*-class battleships.

Source B

Germany is a young and growing empire with a worldwide commerce that is rapidly expanding … Germany must have a powerful fleet to protect that commerce and its many interests in even the most distant seas. Germany expects those interests to go on growing, and must be able to champion them resolutely in any quarter of the globe. Our horizons stretch far away …

Kaiser Wilhelm II speaking in 1908.

Source C

POKER AND TONGS;
OR, HOW WE'VE GOT TO PLAY THE GAME.
KAISER. "I GO THREE *DREADNOUGHTS*."
JOHN BULL. "WELL, JUST TO SHOW THERE'S NO ILL-FEELING, I RAISE YOU THREE."

A *Punch* cartoon of 1908 about the naval race between Britain and Germany.

⋯⫶ Activity

Create a timeline showing the naval race between Britain and Germany using the table below to help you.

Year	British policy	German policy
1889	Britain adopts the 'two power standard'	
1895		
1898		
1904		
1906		
1908		
1909		

1　Why was *HMS Dreadnought* such a revolutionary battleship?

2　Read Source B carefully. What reasons does the Kaiser give for needing a powerful navy?

3　How important was the arms race in increasing tensions in Europe before 1914?

DID THE EUROPEAN POWERS MAKE PLANS FOR WAR?

In the years before the First World War, the European powers each created plans for war, so that they would be ready to fight immediately should war break out.

The Schlieffen Plan

The Franco-Russian Alliance alarmed Germany – it meant that, should war break out, Germany would have to fight a war against both Russia and France. Germany would therefore have to fight a war on two fronts – against France to the west, and Russia to the east. This would stretch German resources to the full and make it very difficult to win.

By 1905, the German Army's Chief of Staff, Count von Schlieffen, had drawn up plans for a war on two fronts. Schlieffen stated that Germany must defeat France speedily before Russia was ready to fight. He based his plan on several assumptions:

- Germany could defeat France in a few weeks with sufficient troops.

- Since France had strengthened its defences along the border with Germany, it would be easier for Germany to attack from the north, through the neutral countries of Belgium and Luxembourg. Schlieffen believed that these countries would offer no resistance to German troops.

- The French would probably attack Germany along the French-German border, so Germany must have enough troops there to launch a counter-offensive.

- It would take Russia about six weeks to fully **mobilise** its army.

- For the first six weeks of fighting, only a small army would be needed to fight against Russia; the rest of the German army could be used to defeat France.

This Schlieffen Plan was later modified. But although it was altered, most historians believe it remained the basis for Germany's plans for a possible future war.

Glossary

mobilise: to get ready to fight.

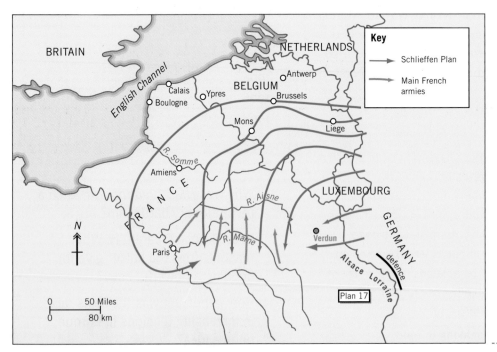

The Schlieffen Plan.

Plan 17

After 1871, the French planned a war of revenge against Germany to win back Alsace and Lorraine. They fortified the border with Germany and built a ring of forts around the historically important city of Verdun to stop a possible German attack. By 1913, the French had drawn up Plan 17. By this plan, France would launch a massive attack over the German border and into Lorraine. This plan ignored the possibility that the Germans would attack the north of France, and so northern France was left undefended.

Did other countries have plans for war?

Almost all European powers created war plans of their own. These included details of how and when troops, equipment and supplies would be transported by rail. However, once a war started, it would be very difficult to make changes without wrecking the plans altogether. One historian referred to this as 'war by timetable'.

1 Explain what is meant by 'war on two fronts'.

2 Why did Germany fear war on two fronts after 1894?

3 How did Count von Schlieffen plan to avoid fighting a war on two fronts?

4 Did the existence of war plans make a European war more or less likely? Why? You could discuss this question with a partner.

... IN CONCLUSION

- ■ Increased tension in Europe led to an arms race.
- ■ Germany and France built up their armies.
- ■ Britain and Germany took part in a 'naval race'.
- ■ Military leaders drew up war plans, which detailed what their armed forces would do if war started.
- ■ The German war plan was designed to fight a war on two fronts.

PRACTISE YOUR ENQUIRY SKILLS

How valuable are Sources A (page 20) and C (page 21) as evidence of an arms race between the Great Powers in the years before 1914?

6 THE BALKANS: FLASHPOINT FOR WAR!

How did tensions increase in the Balkans?

What's it all about?

In this section you will learn:

- ···▷ how developments in the Balkans between 1908 and 1913 had important consequences
- ···▷ how Serbia had become a powerful Slav nation by 1914
- ···▷ about Serbian ambitions for more land.

AUSTRIA TAKES OVER BOSNIA!

In 1878, Austrian troops occupied Bosnia, although it remained part of the Turkish Empire. Very few people in Bosnia were happy about this. Serbians were also against the occupation, because they wanted Bosnia to unite with Serbia.

In 1908, the Austrians decided to **annex** Bosnia. Serbia hoped that Russia, as the largest Slav nation, would come to the rescue. However, Russia was unable to do anything to help Serbia after suffering severe losses in the Russo-Japanese War (1904–5).

Glossary

annex: to take over completely.

Source A

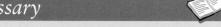

1. Why was Serbia angry about the annexation of Bosnia?

2. Explain why the Russians could not help Serbia in 1908.

THE BALKAN WARS, 1912–13

Russia was keen to support the new countries in the Balkans (see Chapter 2, pages 10–11) and therefore helped to set up the Balkan League of Serbia, Greece and Bulgaria in 1912. The League soon declared war on the Turks. In the First Balkan War (1912), Turkey lost almost all its lands in Europe, retaining only Constantinople (modern-day Istanbul).

Alarmed by the growing strength of the Balkan states, the major European powers organised a conference in London to discuss the future of the Balkans. The result of this conference was the Treaty of London, signed in 1913. The treaty gave Bulgaria most of the land that had been won from Turkey. To prevent Serbia from having direct access to the Mediterranean Sea and becoming too powerful, a new state, Albania, was created.

A French cartoon from 1908. The Austrian Emperor (left) grabs Bosnia from Turkey while the ruling prince of Bulgaria makes himself king and breaks the remaining connections Bulgaria had with Turkey.

The members of the Balkan League soon quarrelled among themselves about who should have the lands seized from Turkey. A Second Balkan War (1913) ended in defeat for Bulgaria, which was forced to give up much of the land it had acquired at the end of the First Balkan War. Serbia gained most from the two Balkan Wars – by the end of 1913, Serbia was stronger than ever.

The Balkans in 1914.

WHAT HAPPENED NEXT IN THE BALKANS?

As Serbia grew more powerful, the Serbs talked openly about uniting all Serbs, including those living in Austrian-ruled Bosnia, under the leadership of Serbia. In Austria, there was a growing fear of Serb nationalism: it seemed to threaten the existence of the Austro-Hungarian Empire.

■ If Austria-Hungary went to war with Serbia, would Russia come to the aid of its Slav neighbours?

■ If Russia came to the aid of Serbia, would Germany support Austria-Hungary?

The situation in the Balkans created dangerous tensions in Europe. Would another Balkan War involve the Great Powers?

1   Describe the results of the Balkan Wars, 1912–13.

2   Explain why many people believed there would be another war in the Balkans. Use Source C and your own knowledge to answer the question.

Source B

By the beginning of 1914, the Austro-Hungarian government had been driven to the conclusion that a military confrontation leading to the crushing of Serbia was absolutely necessary if the Habsburg Empire was to survive.

A modern historian writing in 2002.

Source C

There are no illusions about the importance of events in the Balkans for the future of the Austro-Hungarian Empire. With amazement and worry, we watch the sudden growth of Serbia and on all lips is the worried question: what is to become of Austria-Hungary? Will it be possible to keep the 7 million southern Slavs within the Austrian Empire if the government does not take vigorous action against Serbian claims?

A German journalist writing in November 1912.

Source D

The time will come when the patience of Austria-Hungary in the face of Serb provocation will end. Then there will be no alternative but for Austria-Hungary to attack Serbia. I can tell you, with the Kaiser's approval, that, if Austria were to attack Serbia and Russia were to mobilise, Germany too would mobilise her entire army, which for her means at once opening hostilities against France and Russia.

Count von Moltke, German Chief of Staff, in a letter to the Austrian Chief of Staff in 1909.

Source E

If Austria-Hungary demands something, then the Serbian government must give in. If it does not, the capital, Belgrade, will be bombarded and occupied. Of this, you can be sure, that I stand behind you, and am ready to draw the sword if ever Austria's action makes it necessary!

The German Kaiser, speaking to the head of the Austrian government in 1913.

... IN CONCLUSION

- Austria annexed Bosnia in 1908 and this angered Serbia.
- As a result of the Balkan Wars (1912–13), Serbia became more powerful.
- Future problems in the Balkans were likely to involve the Great Powers.
- Austria saw Serbia as a threat; Germany seemed to be prepared to support Austria.
- Russia had let the Slavs down in 1908 and would not want to do so again.

PRACTISE YOUR ENQUIRY SKILLS

1   Read Source C (page 25) carefully. What does the author think about the situation in the Balkans in 1912? Explain your answer with reference to the source.

2   To what extent do Sources D and E above agree about the situation in the Balkans?

FROM ASSASSINATION IN THE BALKANS TO EUROPEAN WAR

How did a murder spark the First World War?

What's it all about?

In June 1914, the heir to the Austro-Hungarian throne was assassinated while visiting the capital of Bosnia. This sparked off a process that led to war throughout Europe within a matter of weeks.

THE ASSASSINATION OF ARCHDUKE FERDINAND

On 28 June 1914, Archduke Franz Ferdinand, the heir to the Austro-Hungarian throne, and his wife Sophie visited Sarajevo, the capital of Bosnia.

28 June was a significant date for the Serbs. On that day, over 500 years earlier, Serbia had been defeated by the Turks and had lost its independence. When Archduke Ferdinand's visit was announced, a group of Serb nationalists living in Bosnia began to plot how they would exploit the occasion as dramatically as possible. The Black Hand, a Serbian secret organisation, provided training for several young Bosnians who were prepared to assassinate the Archduke.

On 28 June, security in Sarajevo was lax and, unknown to the police, seven assassins were waiting in the crowd. The Archduke and his wife travelled in an open car, accompanied by the local governor. There were four other cars in the motorcade.

One of the assassins threw a hand grenade at the car carrying the Archduke. The driver saw it coming and accelerated, so that the grenade glanced off the back of the Archduke's car and damaged the car behind, severely injuring two of the occupants. When Franz Ferdinand reached the Town Hall, he insisted on visiting the hospital where the injured men were being treated.

On the way to the hospital, the driver took a wrong turning and slowed down to reverse the car. At that moment, one of the assassins, nineteen-year-old Gavrilo Princip, came out of a local café, believing the whole plot to have failed. Seeing the Archduke's car almost stationary, he seized the opportunity, drew a pistol and shot the Archduke and his wife from close range. Both died shortly afterwards. The Black Hand had succeeded in their plot to assassinate the heir to the Austro-Hungarian Empire.

Source A

A *Punch* cartoon of July 1914.

THE POWER BEHIND.

1   In your own words, describe the events of 28 June 1914.

2   Why was the Archduke unpopular with so many Bosnian Serbs?

HOW DID THE ASSASSINATION LEAD TO WAR?

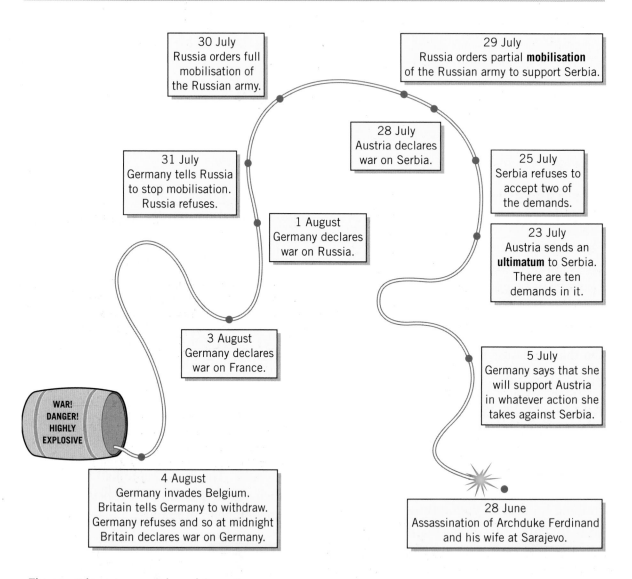

30 July
Russia orders full mobilisation of the Russian army.

29 July
Russia orders partial **mobilisation** of the Russian army to support Serbia.

28 July
Austria declares war on Serbia.

25 July
Serbia refuses to accept two of the demands.

31 July
Germany tells Russia to stop mobilisation. Russia refuses.

1 August
Germany declares war on Russia.

23 July
Austria sends an **ultimatum** to Serbia. There are ten demands in it.

3 August
Germany declares war on France.

5 July
Germany says that she will support Austria in whatever action she takes against Serbia.

WAR! DANGER! HIGHLY EXPLOSIVE

4 August
Germany invades Belgium. Britain tells Germany to withdraw. Germany refuses and so at midnight Britain declares war on Germany.

28 June
Assassination of Archduke Ferdinand and his wife at Sarajevo.

The countdown to war, July and August 1914.

Glossary

ultimatum: a final warning requiring a government to agree to certain conditions, or else action will be taken against them.

mobilisation: preparation for war.

Why did Britain declare war on Germany?

In 1839, Britain had signed an international treaty guaranteeing that Belgium would always remain a neutral country. When Germany invaded Belgium, on 4 August 1914, Britain entered the war to defend Belgium's right to be neutral.

···∴ *Activity*

Working in groups, prepare the main front-page stories for a national newspaper published on 4 August 1914 in one of the following capital cities:

■ London   ■ Berlin   ■ Paris   ■ Vienna   ■ Saint Petersburg.

In your newspaper you should:

■ outline the events since 28 June which have led to war

■ explain why the country in which your newspaper is published is now at war

■ consider where the blame lies for the outbreak of war.

If you have access to the Internet, search for a suitable picture or photograph from 1914 for the front page.

WHO WAS RESPONSIBLE FOR THE FIRST WORLD WAR?

In 1919, the defeated nations, Germany and Austria-Hungary, were blamed for starting the war. Was this view justified? Many people have since tried to find a satisfactory explanation for the First World War. Some of the explanations for the First World War are:

> Germany was responsible – she encouraged Austria to attack Serbia.

> Germany was clearly planning for war. Many people in Germany felt that a war would solve Germany's social problems and unite the people.

> Britain did not make it clear that she would intervene if the Germans invaded Belgium. By failing to make this clear, Britain must take some of the blame.

> Austria-Hungary was responsible. They wanted a war with Serbia because they saw Serb nationalism as a threat to the Austro-Hungarian Empire. War with Serbia would mean war with Russia.

> All of the countries involved must share the responsibility. In 1914, war seemed an exciting prospect, and schools in every country taught children to believe in the greatness of their nation. Popular newspapers spread the belief that war was a way of proving a country's prestige. The arms race and alliances had existed for years.

> In 1914, many people wanted peace but European governments believed they could achieve more through war than negotiation. They also believed that their status as a Great Power was at risk if they did not fight.

···⫶ Activity

1   Working with a partner, try to find evidence from the textbook to support each of the six points of view described on page 29. You could look for additional evidence in the school or departmental library, or on the Internet. Present your findings using the following table:

	Who was responsible?	Evidence
View 1		

2   Which view do you find most convincing? Why does it convince you?

··· IN CONCLUSION

···⫶
■ On 28 June 1914, the heir to the Austrian throne, Archduke Franz Ferdinand, was assassinated in Bosnia.

■ The Austrians blamed Serbia for the assassination and, after issuing an ultimatum, Austria declared war on Serbia.

■ Within six weeks of the assassination, the Great Powers of Europe were at war.

PRACTISE YOUR ENQUIRY SKILLS

1   What was the attitude of the cartoonist who drew Source A (page 27) towards the crisis in the Balkans?

2   Look at Source A (page 27). Which country is shown as:

■ the eagle

■ the cock

■ the bear?

EXTENDED WRITING PRACTISE

How important was Germany's role in the events leading to war in 1914? You should consider:

■ the part Germany played in the events leading to war

■ other factors that contributed to the outbreak of war.

You should include a conclusion that provides a balanced answer to the question.

8 THE EXPERIENCE OF WAR ON THE WESTERN FRONT

What was the impact of war in 1914?

What's it all about?

With the outbreak of war in 1914, many people regarded it as an exciting adventure. In western Europe, the invading German armies made progress at first, but by the autumn of 1914 they had ground to a stop. Troops began to dig defensive trenches and the war reached a stalemate.

REACTIONS TO THE OUTBREAK OF WAR

At the start of the war, the Germans expected a swift victory. France and Britain, too, believed that the war would be 'over by Christmas'. Both sides shared the belief that the war would be won, or lost, on the **Western Front**.

Source A

A photograph of German troops setting off for war in August 1914, in a cheerful mood. Someone has chalked onto the side of the truck 'Ausflug nach Paris' (Excursion to Paris) and 'Auf Wiedersehen auf den Boulevard' (See you again on the streets of Paris).

Glossary

Western Front: the area of fighting in France and Belgium during the First World War.

THE PROGRESS OF THE WAR IN 1914

Nearly a million German soldiers crossed the Belgian border in August 1914, in line with the Schlieffen Plan (see page 22). Then the plan started to go wrong. At Liege, the Belgians put up strong resistance and, instead of taking the fortress in two days as Schlieffen had planned, it was ten days before it fell to the Germans.

The British Expeditionary Force (BEF) was ready to fight by mid August, and the troops were welcomed when they landed in France. On 24 August, the BEF was in action at Mons, where the rapid rifle fire of Britain's professional soldiers led the Germans to believe that they were up against machine-gun fire. The BEF was, however, unable to hold its position and eventually joined the French in what became known as 'The Great Retreat'.

Source B

The whole of Boulogne turned out to cheer us on with shouts of 'Huway, huway!' and 'Vive l'Angleterre' and 'Les Allemands, Wuh!' followed by a sign with the hand drawn across the neck as if to cut it. They were most enthusiastic and at a halt brought us plums, beer and water.

From the diary of a soldier with the Middlesex Regiment, who landed at Boulogne, France, in August 1914.

The Battle of the Marne, 5–10 September 1914

By early September, the German army had crossed the River Marne in France. By this time, they could see Paris but had advanced so fast that it was difficult to keep supply lines open. The German First Army had been ordered to move to the south-east instead of encircling Paris from the west as had originally been planned. As the Battle of the Marne commenced, a British spotter plane noticed a 30-mile gap between the First and Second German armies. British and French troops moved into this gap, forcing the Germans back.

Both sides soon started to dig into defensive positions so they could hold the gains that they had made. Gradually, these defensive positions extended towards the Channel as the armies tried unsuccessfully to outflank each other in the 'race to the sea'. Instead of a war of movement, both sides had reached a **stalemate**.

The French army suffered 800,000 casualties in the first four months of the war, and the BEF forces that had landed in France in August had almost ceased to exist. The German army also suffered appalling losses – and this was just the beginning.

Glossary

stalemate: when neither side in a war can advance.

The opening months of the war on the Western Front.

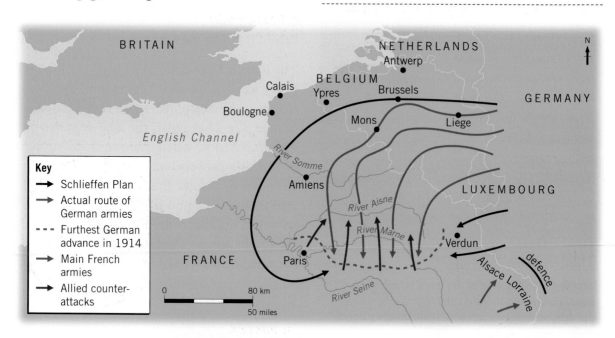

Key
→ Schlieffen Plan
→ Actual route of German armies
--- Furthest German advance in 1914
→ Main French armies
→ Allied counter-attacks

Source C

Scots Guards, autumn 1914. This early trench is little more than a basic defensive ditch. The generals believed that a war of movement would start again in the spring.

How did people react to the declaration of war?

Many people were excited when war was declared in 1914. French and German **reservists** hurried to join their regiments while in Britain, young men rushed to volunteer, even lying about their age so they could join the army immediately, not wanting to miss out on the adventure. Nearly 100 years later, however, some historians have questioned whether this feeling of enthusiasm was as widespread as was once thought. The sources and information on page 34 suggest that people experienced many different feelings in the early months of the war.

Glossary

reservists: men with military training not currently in the army.

Source D

On 14 September, the Germans were exhausted, could march no more; they scratched holes in the ground, set up machine guns. To everyone's amazement, the advancing Allies hesitated, stopped. One man with a machine gun, protected by mounds of earth, was more powerful than the advancing masses. Trench warfare had begun. The war of movement ended when men dug themselves in.

A historian writing in 1963.

1 Write a paragraph explaining why the Schlieffen Plan failed. Use the text and the maps on pages 22 and 32 to help you.

2 Why did trench warfare develop on the Western Front? Use Sources C and D to answer this question.

Source E

In Germany, nearly half a million people participated in anti-war demonstrations in July 1914.

A modern historian writing in 1998.

Source F

I adore war! It's like a big picnic without being as pointless as a picnic. I've never been so well or happy. No one grumbles at one for being dirty.

Julian Grenfell, writing in September 1914.

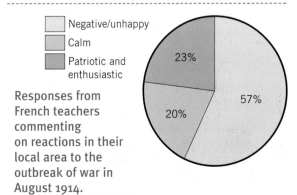

Negative/unhappy
Calm
Patriotic and enthusiastic

23%
57%
20%

Responses from French teachers commenting on reactions in their local area to the outbreak of war in August 1914.

Source G

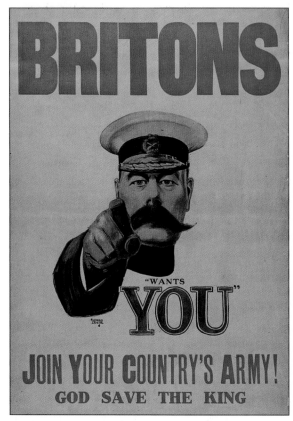

Lord Kitchener, the British Secretary of State for War and a national hero, points the finger – a recruitment poster of 1914.

Source H

France, 1 August 1914

The village bell rang to announce mobilisation. Nobody spoke for a while. Some were out of breath, others were dumb with shock. 'What can it mean? What's going to happen to us?' asked all the women. Wives, children, husbands – all were overcome with anguish and emotion. The wives clung to the arms of their husbands. The children, seeing their mothers weeping, started to cry too. All around us was alarm and consternation. What a disturbing scene!

A French schoolteacher comments on reactions to the outbreak of war.

Source I

Unemployment did not fill the ranks of Kitchener's army, popular sentiment did. The protection of 'little Belgium', the defence of the Empire, the need to be seen doing one's military duty alongside the men of one's district or village: these may sound like outworn clichés but in 1914 they had force and substance in the minds of ordinary people.

A modern historian.

Source J

Industries, frightened by the economic uncertainty caused by the war, reacted by cutting jobs. Nearly 500,000 men were made redundant by the end of August, and many more were forced to work part-time. The very first rush of recruits was dominated by the sort that had always volunteered for the army, namely the young, unskilled, unemployed and desperate.

From a modern history book, 1996.

Source K

I enlisted on 9 September 1914 in Cambuslang. I really did not go with the intention of joining up. I just went to see the fun, because whenever a lad went to join up, the crowd would give him a hearty cheer. So after standing around for a while I must have got carried away. So in went another recruit – me! I was duly sworn in and became a soldier of the king in the Queen's Own Cameron Highlanders.

A young Scottish soldier.

···⫶ *Activity*

1   Copy the table below into your notes. Working in pairs, discuss Sources E–K and the pie chart. Decide which attitude is reflected in each source.

Some sources may reflect more than one attitude. The first one has been done for you.

Attitude towards the war	Evidence
Opposed to war	Source E
In search of adventure	
Patriotic reasons for joining up	
Economic reasons for joining up	
Anxious about the future	
Influenced by other people	

2   'Everywhere in Europe, the outbreak of war was greeted with enthusiasm.' How far do you agree with this view?

Write a short essay in answer to this question using the information you have gathered in the table above.

··· IN CONCLUSION

··⫶   ▪ The war in western Europe began as a war of movement; by November, the war had reached stalemate and trench warfare began.

  ▪ Many people greeted the war with enthusiasm; some were more fearful about the future.

PRACTISE YOUR ENQUIRY SKILLS

1   How useful is Source A (page 31) as evidence of German attitudes towards war in August 1914?

2   What does Source B (page 32) reveal about French and British feelings towards war in August 1914?

3   In what ways do Sources I and J (page 34) differ about the reasons why men rushed to volunteer for the British army?

9 TRENCH WARFARE ON THE WESTERN FRONT

What was life like in the trenches?

What's it all about?

Life in the trenches was hard – the lives of the frontline soldiers were constantly at risk. Because it was easier to defend than to attack, 'going over the top' was highly dangerous. Military planners believed that they were fighting a war of **attrition** and that they had to kill or injure as many of the enemy as possible.

THE SYSTEM OF TRENCHES

When the soldiers on the Western Front dug in to defend their positions in the autumn of 1914, no one imagined that the lines of trenches would remain virtually unchanged until the spring of 1918. Both sides recognised that although battles raged on other fronts, the war would be lost or won on the Western Front. Vast numbers of men and resources were used to strengthen the system of trenches, thus making it even harder for the enemy to achieve the **breakthrough** that might lead to victory. The hastily dug, defensive ditches (see Source C on page 33) soon became elaborate trench systems.

British and French trenches usually consisted of a frontline trench, a support trench and then a reserve line, connected by communication trenches designed to protect soldiers as they went up the line. In Flanders, Belgium, the ground was so wet that it flooded immediately if soldiers dug down, so the troops constructed above-ground sandbag defences known as 'breastworks'.

The Germans thought of their trenches as reasonably permanent and so they tended to be better constructed than those of the British, often including reinforced concrete shelters, or dugouts, which were in some cases equipped with electric light and furniture.

Glossary

attrition: wearing down the enemy.

breakthrough: the destruction of the enemy's trenches so that troops could pass through the gap in the defences and force the enemy to retreat.

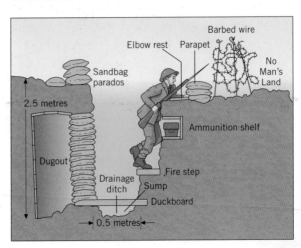

A typical frontline trench.

Features of the trench system

A typical frontline trench on the Western Front. The enemy's frontline was only about 200 metres away – often less.

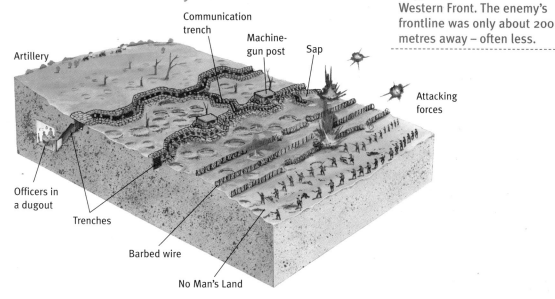

Communication trench

Machine-gun post

Sap

Artillery

Attacking forces

Officers in a dugout

Trenches

Barbed wire

No Man's Land

- **Saps** were used as listening posts so that troops could be alerted to the possibility of enemy patrols into No Man's Land at night, or the even greater danger posed by enemy miners who might be attempting to blow up a section of the frontline.

- The zigzag lines of the trenches were created by **traverses**, which made it difficult for the enemy to capture a part of the line and then fire along a lengthy section of the trench. Traverses also helped to limit the effects of direct hits from **grenades** or **mortars**.

Glossary

saps: short trenches leading to a listening post or a machine gunner's position.

traverse: a right angle in a trench.

grenade: a small bomb thrown by hand or shot from a rifle.

mortar: a short stumpy tube through which explosives are fired.

Shells could destroy whole sections of the frontline trenches when the gunner's range was accurate. Heavy shelling also destroyed buildings and vegetation, leaving great shell holes in No Man's Land and creating a nightmare landscape of mud, bare tree stumps and rubble. When farm drainage ditches were destroyed, the land became waterlogged, creating a quagmire through which it was almost impossible to pass.

> Explain the significance of each of the following: machine-gun posts; dugouts; barbed wire; communication trenches; duckboards; latrine saps; No Man's Land.

FRONTLINE DUTY

Even when a particular sector of the trenches was 'quiet', the frontline soldiers lived and worked in appalling conditions. The trenches often flooded and it was impossible to keep dry. The daily routine was monotonous as well as dangerous. Enemy snipers were always on the watch for signs of activity that would suggest a target.

The daily routine

- The order to 'stand to' was given at daybreak. Everyone had to be awake and on guard. This was the most likely time for the enemy to shell the frontlines. The British called this regular early morning firing 'the daily hate'.

- 'Stand down' meant the most dangerous time was over – the men could get breakfast. Some soldiers remained on guard while the others ate.

- Duties, or 'fatigues', filled much of the day. These included **sentry duty**, filling sandbags, repairing trenches, fetching supplies from behind the lines. Otherwise, soldiers passed the time cleaning their rifles or kit, writing letters or getting some sleep.

- As evening fell, there was another period of 'stand to'.

- When 'stand down' was called at night, a period of great activity began. Patrols crawled into No Man's Land to get information about the enemy. Wiring parties repaired the barbed wire in front of the trenches while others attempted to cut the enemy's wire. A raiding party might attempt to capture prisoners from the enemy's trenches. Flares were used to light the night sky so that enemy patrols could be spotted.

Glossary

sentry duty: the watch or guard kept by a soldier.

Tommies: British soldiers.

Behind the lines

Soldiers spent about eight days at the front, followed by a longer spell 'behind the lines'. Although there was always work to do, it was also a time to relax and try to forget the dangers of the trenches for a while.

Food was better behind the lines and there was the possibility of buying extra food locally. Few British soldiers could speak French, but the army provided them with a few essential phrases and many **Tommies** soon learned that gestures and a few francs would get them eggs, coffee or cheese.

As well as training and routine repairs, there was the chance to play football, or perhaps see a film at a field cinema. Soldiers also put on their own entertainment – pantomimes were popular, as were more sporting activities such as 'stretcher bearer competitions' and bareback racing on mules.

Source A

A postcard created for troops on the Western Front by the British Expeditionary Force.

Source B

The Red Lamp was situated at the end of a cul-de-sac. Right on the dot of 6 pm a red lamp over the doorway of the brothel was switched on. There was a roar from the troops, accompanied by a forward lunge towards the entrance … Madame in charge, a big, black haired woman with a massive bosom, stood at the foot of the stairway, palm outstretched: one franc for madame, one franc for the dame.

George Coppard describes a brothel for British soldiers in France.

1   How useful do you think British soldiers would have found French Made Easy (Source A)?

2   Source B describes a brothel for ordinary soldiers. There were separate establishments for officers. What does this tell us about attitudes at that time?

'Going over the top'

All soldiers dreaded the order to attack. 'Going over the top' meant scrambling out of the frontline trench and advancing across No Man's Land in the face of enemy fire. In doing so, the attacker was liable to be shot down by machine-gun fire or killed by an enemy shell within moments of leaving the relative safety of the trenches. Many soldiers died entangled in the barbed wire, while thousands of injured soldiers crawled into shell holes in No Man's Land where they died slowly and painfully, or endured an agonising wait before a party of stretcher bearers could risk venturing out to rescue them.

A war of attrition

Despite the dangers, generals on both sides continued to order their men to attack the enemy's trenches. At first they were prepared to risk the lives of thousands of their soldiers in the belief that **'a big push'** on one sector of the trenches might force the enemy to retreat along a whole section of the front. However, as the stalemate continued, it became clear that these attacks were not working and that there would be no easy breakthrough. Instead, generals developed the idea of a war of attrition. When they attacked, they knew many men would be killed or wounded, but they hoped to inflict such heavy casualties on the enemy that eventually they would 'wear down' their opponents.

Glossary

a big push: a major attack on a particular section of the enemy's trenches.

Source C

A photograph showing Canadian soldiers 'going over the top' in October 1916.

Source D

Zero hour came and I swarmed up the ladder … Occasionally a shell would burst and some poor fellow would be torn asunder. Men dropped out just as you read in books or see in pictures; in the midst of the great turmoil, there was a strange silence. The excitement of the battle was still on me then – I wanted to push on and on. One poor chap's brains were blown out less than a yard off.

A British soldier recalls his experiences on the Western Front, 1916.

1   Explain why it was so dangerous to 'go over the top'.

2   Why were soldiers ordered to 'go over the top' even though it was known that casualties would be high?

LIFE IN THE TRENCHES

⋯◈ Activity

1   Using the information and sources on pages 38–40, produce an uncensored report on life in the trenches for a British newspaper. The title of your report is: 'Twenty-four hours with our boys at the front.'

■   Look in the library or on the Internet for more primary sources relating to trench life.

■   You could use a word processor or PowerPoint to present your findings.

2   You have been told not to include anything in your report that is bad for morale back home in Britain. What should you leave out of your report?

Source E

Rats bred by the tens of thousands … When we were sleeping in dugouts, the things ran over us, played about, mated and fouled our scraps of food, their young squeaking incessantly. Empty tins of all kinds were flung away over the top on both sides of the trench. During brief moments of quiet at night, one could hear a continuous rattle of tins moving against each other. The rats were turning them over.

George Coppard recalls life in the trenches.

Source F

Rations were tied in sandbags and consisted, usually, of bread, hard biscuits, tinned meat (bully) in 12 oz tins, tinned jam, tinned butter, sugar and tea, pork and beans (baked beans with a piece of pork fat on top), cigarettes and tobacco. Sometimes we got a sort of Irish stew in tins that could be quickly heated over a charcoal brazier. When it was possible to have a cookhouse within easy reach of trenches, fresh meat, bacon, vegetables, flour, etc., would be sent up and the cooks could produce reasonably good meals.

A soldier, interviewed about the war in 1978.

Source G

Many men got trench feet and trench fever. With trench fever, a fellow had a high temperature, you could see he had. It wasn't dysentery but he had constant diarrhoea, it left him weak and listless. Trench feet was owing to the wet soaking through your boots. In many cases your toes nearly rotted off.

A British officer speaking about the war. Trench fever was spread by lice and soldiers would regularly examine their clothes for them.

Source H

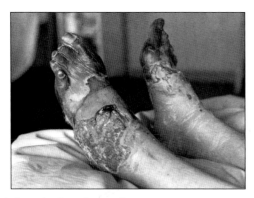

Trench foot. In the winter of 1914–15, over 20,000 men in the British army were treated for trench foot. By the end of 1915, men were ordered to change their socks twice a day and to cover their feet in a grease made of whale oil.

Source I

Just a few words about your last parcel. *Cigarettes – capital* but don't send any more until I ask you to. *Toffee, condensed milk, candles, rice and potted meat;* the toffee, milk, rice and one candle have all gone. The Oxo cubes will be very nice to augment my soup with no doubt … That pastry of your own make was a perfect success.

A letter from Bert Bailey to his wife. He was killed a few hours after writing it.

Source J

I do not think anyone can understand the wearisome monotony of fighting unless he has spent a night in the trenches. It is deadly dull, and the dullness, more than the discomfort, is what strikes me. Today I am covered in mud, having fallen in the dark into a shell hole.

Robert MacFie, a soldier with the Liverpool Scottish.

Source K

It was early morning and stand to was over. The fire was going nicely and the bacon was sizzling. I was sitting on the firestep and just as I was about to tuck in Bill crashed to the ground. I'll never forget the sound of that shot … I rushed round the traverse and yelled, 'Pass the word for the stretcher bearers!' We waited for them to come and for decency's sake put some bandages round Bill's head to hide the mess. We carried him to the first aid post. On getting back to the frontline, we were ravenous with hunger. My bacon and bread were on the firestep but covered with dirt and bits of Bill's brain.

George Coppard describes his experiences in the trenches.

... IN CONCLUSION

- A complex system of trenches developed on the Western Front.
- Frontline conditions were unpleasant and very dangerous.
- Soldiers spent a considerable amount of time 'behind the lines'.
- Casualties were very high when men 'went over the top'.
- Generals accepted that they were fighting a war of attrition.

PRACTISE YOUR ENQUIRY SKILLS

1 Which do you consider more valuable as evidence about the trenches: the diagram on page 36 or Source C (page 39)? Give reasons for your answer.

2 How far do Sources C and D (pages 39 and 40) agree about what happened when soldiers 'went over the top'?

10   1916: SLAUGHTER ON THE WESTERN FRONT

What were the major battles of 1916?

What's it all about?

Fighting on the Western Front became even more intense in 1916, as both sides tried to achieve a breakthrough. The German attack at Verdun, and the joint British and French attack at the Somme, led to appallingly high casualties without any significant achievements.

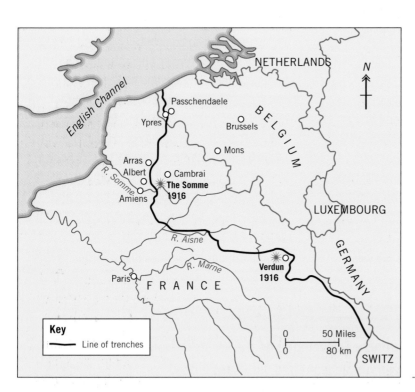

The Western Front in 1916.

VERDUN: THE WORLD'S GREATEST BATTLE?

Von Falkenhayn's plan

Early in 1916 the German Chief of Staff, General von Falkenhayn, decided to attack the French frontline around Verdun. Massive forts had been built in the hills around Verdun and the Germans believed that the French would do everything they could to defend these fortifications.

Falkenhayn believed that many French soldiers would die defending Verdun, such that 'the forces of France will bleed to death'. He believed that Germany would then have only Britain to fight in the west.

By mid February, Falkenhayn had assembled a huge army and over 1200 field guns along a 13 km section of the front. However, the German attack was delayed because of bad weather and the French were able to bring up additional reinforcements.

The battle begins ...

On 21 February, the bombardment began. The French defences were shelled for nine hours – some 80,000 shells fell on one small area of the front. In the first four days of fighting, the Germans made some progress and, when Fort Douaumont fell, it seemed that the way to Verdun was open.

At this point, a new French commander, General Pétain, was sent to Verdun. A single road into Verdun was kept open so that supplies and men could be transported to the front. By June, vehicles were travelling along this 'Sacred Road' at the rate of one every fourteen seconds. This was the first battle ever in which motor transport played a vital role.

The slaughter at Verdun continued until December. At first, the Germans made some advances but the French counter-attacked in October and recaptured Fort Douaumont. By the time that the fighting ended, 377,000 French soldiers were dead, missing or wounded. German casualties were only slightly fewer, at 337,000.

Source B

I climbed up to the top of the gully. Fort Douaumont was in front of me. I could see across an area of ten square kilometres that had been turned into a uniform desert of brown earth. The men were all so tiny and lost in it that I could hardly see them. A shell fell in the midst of these little things, which moved for a moment, carrying off the wounded – the dead, as unimportant as so many ants, were left behind.

A French soldier writing about Verdun.

Source C

There were about 20 German soldiers. Their faces stared at us like those of shrunken mummies, and their eyes seemed so huge that one saw nothing but eyes. Those eyes, which had not seen sleep for four days and nights, portrayed the vision of death. Was this the dream of glory that I had when I volunteered to march with the Kaiser through the Arc de Triomphe?

A German soldier describing Verdun, 1916.

Source A

Hell by Georges Leroux. Leroux fought with a French camouflage unit at Verdun.

1 Why did the Germans decide to attack at Verdun?

2 What was the result of the nine months of fighting at Verdun?

LIONS LED BY DONKEYS? – THE BATTLE OF THE SOMME

In December 1915, British and French generals started to plan a joint 'push' near the River Somme. They believed the offensive would create a gap in the German lines, enabling cavalry and troops to take advantage of the breakthrough.

The attack was originally to take place in August 1916, but by the spring, the French were under such pressure at Verdun that they asked the British to attack sooner. Eventually, it was decided to attack on 1 July 1916. The French would not be able to contribute as many troops as had been hoped because they were needed at Verdun. However, Britain's new volunteer soldiers – Kitchener's army – were ready to fight, and die, for their country.

What was General Haig's plan?

General Haig was in charge of the battle. According to Haig's plan, the battle would progress in the following way:

- A week-long artillery bombardment by over 1500 guns along a 30 km frontline would destroy German trenches and machine-gun posts before the attack began.
- British spotter planes would relay information about the position of German artillery to British gun crews on the ground so that they could target their fire accurately.
- Shelling would destroy the barbed wire in front of the German trenches.
- With the German trenches and machine-gun posts destroyed, British troops could walk across No Man's Land and capture the enemy's trenches.

What actually happened?

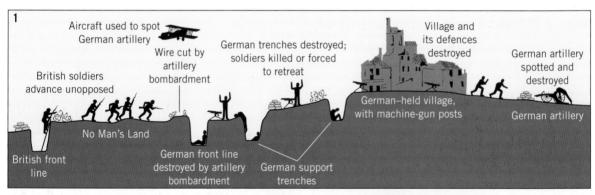

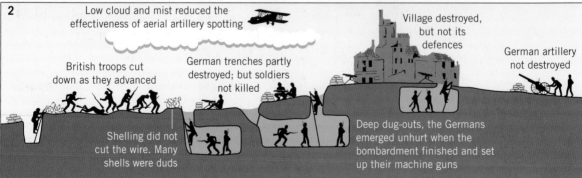

The Battle of the Somme, 1916 – the theory and what actually happened.

The first day of the battle

At 7.30am on 1 July 1916, the barrage of shellfire lifted. All along the front, Allied soldiers fixed their bayonets to their rifles and obeyed the order to 'go over the top'. Carrying packs weighing over 60 lbs, they were ordered to walk steadily forward. One company commander is said to have given each of his four platoons a football so they could compete to see which would be the first to dribble the ball successfully across No Man's Land.

Almost everywhere, the soldiers walked into a hail of German machine-gun fire. The casualties were appalling and nothing could be done to rescue those who were lying wounded in No Man's Land. One Canadian regiment lost 684 out of 752 men in just half an hour.

By the end of the first day of the Battle of the Somme, 20,000 British soldiers had been killed and almost 40,000 wounded. Although there was some progress at certain points, there was no overall breakthrough.

The fighting continues ...

The fighting on the Somme continued until November 1916. By then, British troops had advanced just 9km along a 30km stretch of the front. In all, more than a million men were killed or injured during the five months of fighting at the Somme.

The slaughter of 1916 put an end to any remaining enthusiasm for the war. There was nothing glorious about a slow death in No Man's Land; no excitement in seeing a friend shot down as he tried to make his way across.

1 Using the two diagrams on page 44, explain why the attack on the Somme went so horribly wrong.

2 What were the main results of the Battle of the Somme?

FIELD MARSHAL HAIG

Douglas Haig was born in Edinburgh in 1861. By the time the war started in 1914, he had been in the army for nearly 30 years. In 1915, Haig was appointed Commander-in-Chief of the British Expeditionary Force and in 1917 he was promoted to the rank of Field Marshal. He believed that the cavalry had an important part to play in wars and he underestimated the importance of the machine gun and the tank.

After the war, Haig was made an Earl and was given £100,000, a very large sum of money in those days, as a reward for the way in which he had served his country during the war. He dedicated the rest of his life to setting up charities which looked after ex-soldiers. The most famous of these was the Earl Haig Fund, which exists to this day.

Source D

Field Marshal Haig.

Source E

Hundreds of dead were strung out like wreckage. Quite as many died on the enemy wire as on the ground, like fish caught in the net. They hung there in grotesque postures. Some looked as though they were praying; they had died on their knees and the wire had prevented their fall. From the way the dead were spread out, whether on the wire or lying in front of it, it was clear that there were no gaps in the wire at the time of the attack.

George Coppard describes the slaughter at the Somme, 1 July 1916.

⋯⋗ Activity

Some historians have described General Haig as 'the Butcher of the Somme'. Others point out that Haig was still in charge in 1918 when the Allies won the war and that his tactics worked in the end. They believe that offensives like the Somme were necessary to defeat the Germans.

1   Working in pairs, decide which view of Haig is correct. Use the information box and Sources F to L to help you reach a decision.

2   Explain your decision to the rest of the class.

Source F

It was pure bloody murder. Douglas Haig should have been hanged, drawn and quartered for what he did on the Somme. The cream of British manhood was shattered in less than six hours.

Private P. Smith of the First Border Regiment, July 1916.

Source G

No amount of skill on the part of the higher commanders, no training … will enable victories to be won without the sacrifice of men's lives. The nation must be prepared to see heavy casualty lists.

Written by Haig in June 1916 before the battle began.

Source H

There are still those who argue that the Battle of the Somme should never have been fought and that the gains were not worth the sacrifice. As to whether it was wise or foolish to give battle on the Somme on 1 July 1916, there can surely be only one opinion. To have refused to fight then and there would have meant the abandonment of Verdun to its fate and the breakdown of the cooperation with the French.

From a biography of Haig by Duff Cooper, written in 1936.

Source I

The pressure had been taken off the French at Verdun; the main German army had been held on the Western Front; and the enemy's strength had been very considerably worn down. Any one of these three results justifies the Battle of the Somme. Achieving all three is ample compensation for the splendid efforts of our troops and for the sacrifices made by ourselves and our allies. They have brought us a long step forward towards the final victory of the Allied cause.

Haig writing about the results of the battle in December 1916.

Source J

Haig's nickname was the butcher. He'd think nothing of sending thousands of men to certain death. This was utter waste and disregard for human life and human suffering by the so-called educated classes who ran the country. What a wicked waste of life. I'd hate to be in their shoes when they face their maker.

William Brooks, a private in the British army, speaking in 1993.

Source K

Haig launched an **offensive** which gained too little and cost his own army too much. In spite of the weather, which broke at the end of September, he pursued his aims with the result that little ground was gained and the army suffered heavy losses.

From a recent article about Haig.

Glossary

offensive: an attack.

Source L

A German and a British soldier share a drink of water. The ordinary soldier often believed that the war was pointless and recognised that the 'enemy' was suffering as much as he was.

... IN CONCLUSION

- In 1916, the Germans tried to destroy the French army at Verdun.
- In July 1916, the British attempted a 'breakthrough' on the Somme.
- In both battles, the number of casualties was appallingly high.
- Neither offensive achieved anything significant.
- Some people have criticised General Haig's strategy at the Somme; others point out that Haig's tactics did eventually lead to victory.

PRACTISE YOUR ENQUIRY SKILLS

1   Compare Sources A and B (page 43) as evidence of the effects of the fighting at Verdun.

2   What is the attitude of the German soldier (Source C (page 43)) towards the war?

11 THE TECHNOLOGY OF WAR
How did warfare change?

What's it all about?

New technology affected the way that the First World War was fought. In 1914, military equipment made it easier to defend than to attack, and artillery fire in particular was responsible for many deaths. Later in the war, new developments made it possible to break the deadlock, although there were still many problems to overcome.

NEW WEAPONRY

Until 1914, armies had relied on the cavalry during an attack but two very different inventions – barbed wire and the machine gun – made the cavalry charge impossible during the First World War. In addition, industrialisation meant that vast amounts of weapons and explosives could be produced in a short space of time. As a result, it was now much easier for armies to defend than it was for them to launch a successful attack.

New technologies affected the war in other ways, too. Planes and balloons were used for observing enemy positions. Field telephones and the wireless (radio) were used to pass this information on to those who needed it. Rail and motor transport made it easier to keep armies supplied, and canned food made it possible to feed the soldiers in the trenches, even in winter.

Rifles

Every soldier had a rifle. In the British army this was a Lee Enfield; the German foot soldier most probably had a Mauser. A professional soldier could fire up to fifteen rounds per minute but new recruits, like those who fought at the Somme, could only manage between eight and twelve rounds.

In the trenches, snipers, sometimes working with a 'spotter', used rifles to fire at any sign of movement in the trenches opposite.

Trench mortars and grenades

As well as rifles, frontline soldiers frequently used mortars and grenades.

- Grenades, such as the Mills bomb, were small explosives which were either hand thrown or fired from a rifle. They were used in trench fighting or when a surprise raid was carried out on the enemy's frontline.

- A mortar was a short stumpy tube which fired an explosive at a steep angle so that it would land in the enemy's trench. The German army was well equipped with *minenwerfern* (mine throwers) at the beginning of the war – the British called them 'Minnies'. By 1915, the British army was equipped with Stokes mortars which could fire 22 bombs a minute and had a range of over 1000 metres. Later, mortars could fire almost twice that distance.

Machine guns

In 1914, machine guns were heavy and required a machine-gun crew of up to six men. Because they quickly overheated, they had to have cooling mechanisms attached to them. The British Vickers gun was water-cooled and weighed about 20 kg. Although lighter than some machine guns, it still required six men to operate it and it was difficult to move around the battlefield. For this reason it was increasingly replaced by the lighter and faster-firing Lewis gun after 1915.

Machine guns were mainly used as a defensive weapon. Their rapid rate of fire – a Vickers fired 500 times a minute – meant that a well-located machine-gunner could kill or wound attacking soldiers at an alarming rate, as the British discovered on the first day of the Somme.

> 1 Describe how British soldiers in the trenches used:
>
>   a) Lee Enfield rifles
>
>   b) Stokes mortars.
>
> 2 Why were machine guns mainly used as defensive weapons?

Artillery

The First World War was 'the war of the big guns'. The stalemate on the Western Front meant that long-range guns, capable of firing heavy shells over a great distance, became more and more important. These heavy artillery guns are known as howitzers. By the end of the war, some of these guns could fire 900 kg shells over eighteen km.

Source A

A howitzer firing, Paul Nash.

Artillery fire killed and injured far more soldiers than did machine guns and rifles; shells also churned up the ground around the frontline, making movement almost impossible for both men and equipment.

The 'creeping barrage'

In 1916, the British used a 'creeping barrage' at the Somme. The range of the heavy artillery shelling moved forward as the infantry advanced. In theory, this would destroy German trenches and machine-gun posts so that the British soldiers would not meet with resistance. However, if the artillery got the range wrong they could end up shelling their own soldiers.

In 1917, new artillery techniques were introduced that would help to end the deadlock. Gunners could locate enemy guns more accurately using **'sound-ranging'** and maps based on aerial photography. This meant there was no need for a long bombardment before an attack, which restored the possibility of a surprise attack.

Source B

The soldiers of 1914 faced a battlefield full of flying metal, and battles that had men pitted against machines. Men in the open could not survive. The spade now became the key to safety as troops from all of the warring nations dug trenches to protect themselves from the effects of modern technology. In the new warfare of machine guns, rifles and artillery, it was much easier to defend than it was to attack.

A modern historian writing about the First World War.

Glossary

sound-ranging: a method of establishing the precise location of enemy guns.

⋯⋗ *Activity*

Look at Sources C–G. Decide which sources describes the following:

- rifles
- heavy artillery
- machine guns
- trench mortars and grenades.

For each category, give a reason for your decision, based on the source and the information in the text.

Source C

They drop right into the trench and if you are near you don't stand a chance. It is like a football on a stick. You can see them coming in the daytime and at night they are followed by a trail of sparks.

A soldier describes his experiences on the Western Front.

Source D

We never got anywhere near the Germans. Never got anywhere near them. Our lads was mown down. They were just simply slaughtered. We didn't get anywhere, we never moved from the line, hardly.

A soldier recalls events on the battlefield.

Source E

Explosion by C. R. W. Nevinson, 1916.

Source F

Some of the enemy are only about 60 yards away from our position and the rest about 300 yards. There are snipers all over the place, in the woods and up the trees; and they carry on a hearty old shoot all day.

A soldier describes his experiences of the First World War.

Source G

The show started with a bombardment – you never heard such a din. The enormous shells (our own) came over our heads plainly visible in the sky and burst with a deafening report just in front of us. Incidentally they wiped out dozens of our own men.

A soldier recalls his experiences on the battlefield.

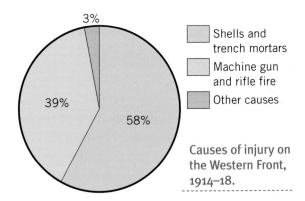

- Shells and trench mortars
- Machine gun and rifle fire
- Other causes

3%
39%
58%

Causes of injury on the Western Front, 1914–18.

GAS

By 1915, all of the countries involved on the Western Front were looking for a way of breaking the deadlock.

The Germans experimented with shells that caused violent sneezing early in the war. At the beginning of 1915, they tried to use tear gas against the Russians, but found that the liquid would not vaporise in the very low winter temperatures. Then, in April 1915, the Germans released over 5000 cylinders of chlorine gas against the British and the Canadians at Ypres, in Belgium.

The cloud of greenish-yellow, choking gas caused such confusion that the Germans were able to advance several kilometres before the Allies managed to stop them.

The following month the British decided to develop chemical weapons, which were used for the first time in September 1915. When the gas had been released, the wind direction changed and the gas blew back over the British trenches. Because the weather was often unpredictable, gas filled shells and mortars had largely replaced cylinders by 1916.

How serious was the threat from gas?

At first, soldiers could do nothing to protect themselves against a gas attack, but it was quickly discovered that a moistened pad placed across the mouth and nose provided some protection. If nothing better was available, the soldiers were instructed to urinate on a piece of cloth and press it to their faces.

By 1916, British troops were issued with a gas helmet – a sort of pull-on hood made of specially treated flannelette. Later that year a small box respirator was issued. This provided much better protection against a range of gases, although it could not protect men from mustard gas.

Source H

I wish those people who talk about going on with this war whatever it costs could see the soldiers suffering from mustard gas poisoning. Great mustard-coloured blisters, blind eyes, all sticky and stuck together, always fighting for breath, with voices a mere whisper, saying that their throats are closing and they know they will choke.

Vera Brittain recalls her impressions as a nurse during the war.

Three main types of gas were used:

- chlorine: a greenish-yellow gas, which formed an acid when it came into contact with the moisture in the lungs, causing fatal damage.
- phosgene: this also destroyed the lungs. Phosgene was invisible and much more deadly than chlorine gas.
- mustard: the most dreaded of the gases used in the First World War. Mustard gas damaged exposed skin, causing huge burn-like blisters and blindness. It also caused internal and external bleeding and was extremely painful.

Gas cylinders used:	88,000
Drums of gas used:	197,000
Gas filled mortars:	178,000
Tons of gas used:	5700

British use of gas during the First World War.

GAS AND INTERNATIONAL LAW

In 1899, Germany had joined other countries to sign an agreement making it illegal to use gas as a weapon. When gas was first used in the First World War, the British were very critical of the Germans. By the end of the war, however, the British had used gas more frequently than the Germans. In 1925, the Geneva Protocol outlawed all chemical and biological weapons. Despite this agreement, nearly a century later, chemical and biological weapons continue to pose a very dangerous threat.

Source I

A painting *Gassed* by John Singer Sargent, 1918–19.

Source J

The effectiveness of anti-gas measures was such that, after April and May 1915, deaths from gas were relatively rare. On the British side, nine per cent of all wounded soldiers treated by medical units from 1915–18 were gas casualties, but of these, only 5899 (3.18 per cent) died.

From a recent history of the First World War, 2000.

1   Why did the British decide to use gas, although it was an illegal weapon?

2   The chart on page 51 shows that the British used gas a great deal during the war. Most British school textbooks concentrate on the German use of gas.

   a) Why do you think this is?

   b) Do you think that it matters when books present information in a one-sided way?

3   Why were gas filled shells and mortars used after 1916?

4   Study Sources H–J.

   Gas did not cause as many deaths as artillery or machine-gun fire. Why was it regarded as such a dangerous weapon?

THE DEVELOPMENT OF THE TANK

In 1902, Frederick Simms, an inventor, demonstrated a 'war-car' that consisted of a motorcar engine surrounded by a bullet-proof shell and equipped with machine guns. At the time, the War Office was not impressed and the 'war car' was abandoned. It was only after the First World War reached a stalemate that some government ministers began to take Simms' ideas more seriously. Winston Churchill, the first Lord of the Admiralty (the government minister responsible for the navy), set up a committee to look into the possibility of building a 'landship' that might help in the search for a breakthrough on the Western Front. The new war machine was given the codename 'tank'.

'Little Willie', the first real tank, was produced in great secrecy. Although it was too slow and could not cross trenches, it showed that tanks could be useful in the future. A new model was designed and, early in 1916, this tank was demonstrated to government ministers. It was hoped the tank could cross No Man's Land and break through the enemy's defences.

150 tanks were ordered. These Mark I tanks were equipped with either a six pound gun (male tanks) or machine guns (female tanks). In either case, the guns were mounted in

sponsons on the sides of the tank. In the autumn of 1916, Mark II and Mark III tanks were ordered for training purposes, and the Mark IV was in use in France by 1917. Later models of the tank followed.

Glossary

sponsons: attachments at the side of the tank which were fitted with guns.

The dawn of a new era in warfare ...

Haig believed that tanks might help break the deadlock during the Battle of the Somme. Early in the morning of 15 September 1916, tanks went into action for the first time. However, because of mechanical problems, only 49 tanks were available and thirteen of these broke down before the attack. Of those that remained, these early tanks were very slow and difficult to manoeuvre, and so became a target for German snipers. Several became stranded in the mud and failed to reach the German lines.

There were too few tanks at the Battle of the Somme to have a significant impact, and Haig was criticised for revealing the secret new weapon too soon. Nevertheless, another thousand tanks were ordered by the British government.

Source K

A poster from 1917 aimed at raising money to build more tanks.

The Battle of Cambrai, 20 November 1917

In November 1917, the first significant tank attack took place. 476 tanks advanced in three waves, driving the Germans from their trenches. This time, the tanks were able to report on their progress because some were equipped with wireless sets. Within a week, the British had advanced over 9 km along an 11 km front. However, problems arose when the tanks made more progress than was expected and there were insufficient troops available to move into the land they had gained. The Germans counter-attacked and the British had to retreat.

Source L

At 6.30 am on 20 November, we heard the sound of tank engines warming up. The tanks, looking like giant toads, became visible against the skyline. Some of the leading tanks carried huge bundles of tightly-bound brushwood, which they dropped when a wide trench was encountered, thus providing a firm base to cross over. It was broad daylight as we crossed No Man's Land and the German frontline. I saw very few wounded coming back, and only a handful of prisoners. The tanks appeared to have busted through any resistance. The enemy wire had been dragged about like old curtains.

George Coppard recalls the impact of tanks during the First World War.

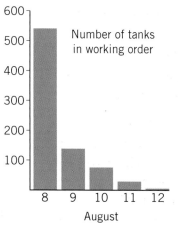

The reliability of tanks during the Battle of Amiens, August 1918.

Source M

Because armoured warfare became a very important element in the Second World War, tanks have been singled out as the decisive weapon of 1918. This is a myth. They bore about as much relation to the tanks of the Second World War as a 1908 Model-T Ford does to a Jaguar.

A modern historian comments on the effectiveness of tank warfare on the Western Front, 1982.

⋯ Activity

1 The tank had advantages and disadvantages as a weapon during the First World War. Copy the table below into your notes and complete it, using information from the text and sources.

Advantages of tanks	Disadvantages of tanks

2 Use the library or the Internet to find out more about the tanks used during the First World War.

3 Working in groups of three or four, create a poster to illustrate the effects of new technology during the First World War.

Your poster should contain the following information:

- ▪ what the new or improved technology was

- ▪ whether it made it easier to defend and why

- ▪ whether it made it easier to attack and why.

You could use a chart like the one below to help you gather information. An example has been completed for you.

Example of new or improved technology	Did it make it easier to defend?	Reasons	Did it make it easier to attack?	Reasons
Machine gun	Yes	Rapid fire made it a killer machine	No	Too heavy to transport quickly

... IN CONCLUSION

- In 1914, technology made it easier for armies to defend than to attack.
- Frontline weapons included rifles, machine guns and mortars.
- Artillery shelling caused the largest number of casualties.
- Gas and tanks were introduced during the war.
- By 1918, improved technology helped to break the deadlock on the Western Front, although tanks remained unreliable in battle.

PRACTISE YOUR ENQUIRY SKILLS

1   How fully does Source B (page 49) explain why fighting was so destructive on the Western Front? Use the source and your own knowledge to answer this question.

2   How fully does Source L (page 53) describe a tank attack during the First World War?

3   To what extent do the graph on page 53 and Source M (page 54) agree about the importance of the tank by the end of the First World War?

12 WORLD WAR

Where else was the First World War fought?

What's it all about?

The First World War was fought in many different parts of the world, so it was truly a 'World War'.

BATTLE FRONTS AROUND THE WORLD

So far this book has concentrated on the fighting on the Western Front. However, there were other important war fronts where Germany and her allies fought against the Entente powers and their allies. These included:

- The Eastern Front, where the Russians fought against Germany and Austria-Hungary.

- The Middle East. At the end of October 1914, Turkey entered the war as an ally of Germany and Austria-Hungary. This led to fierce fighting in the Turkish Empire in the Middle East.

- Northern Italy. In 1915, the Italians entered the war on the side of Britain and France. They hoped to gain Austrian land which they believed should belong to Italy.

- Africa. Germany had several colonies in Africa by 1914; by the beginning of 1918, they had lost all of them except German East Africa.

- The Far East. Japan came into the war in support of her ally, Britain, and took Germany's colonies in the Far East. Australia and New Zealand seized Germany's islands in the Pacific Ocean.

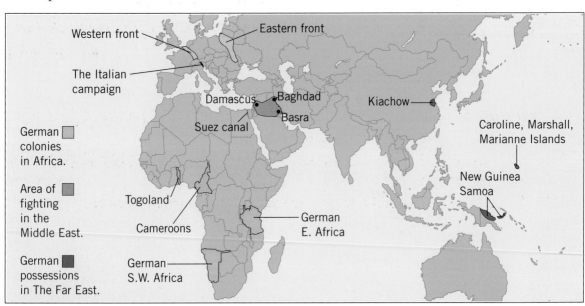

The First World War around the world.

The Eastern Front

Between 1914 and the end of 1917, when Russia withdrew from the war, the Eastern Front saw fighting that was as bitter and desperate as that on the Western Front.

Source A

The entire field of battle, for miles was piled high with corpses, and there weren't enough people or stretchers to clear them away … even to give drink and food to all who were suffering proved impossible. Blood is flowing in endless streams, but there is no other way to fight.

A Russian General, General Brusilov, writing in 1914

Source B

In the book of the Great War, the page on which the Russian losses were written has been torn out. No-one knows the figure. 5 millions or 8 millions? We too have no idea. All we know is that sometimes in our battles with the Russians we had to remove the mounds of enemy corpses in order to get a clear field of fire against fresh assaulting troops.

The German Commander, General von Hindenburg, recalls his experiences on the Eastern Front.

The Middle East

Early in the war, the British landed at Basra to protect oil supplies. Over the next three years, the Turks were gradually driven out of much of the Middle East. In March 1917, the British entered Baghdad and, in December, Jerusalem was taken. On 1 October 1918, the British army entered Damascus. Four weeks later, the Turks surrendered. One of Germany's main allies had been defeated.

Source C

The campaigns in the Middle East were of dubious worth. The forces lost in these 'sideshows' could have made a significant contribution to the Alllied War effort on the Western Front.

The acquisition of lands that were part of the Turkish Empire in the Middle East proved a drain on Britain's diminished resources for years to come. Moreover, Britain in the course of the war made contradictory promises to its Arab and Jewish supporters, which produced unhappy long-term consequences. For both Britain and France, the war in the Middle East left a legacy they could have done without.

Two modern historians, Robin Prior and Trevor Wilson, writing in 1999.

BRITAIN, FRANCE AND THE MIDDLE EAST

- To gain Arab support, the British guaranteed that they would help set up an independent Arab state at the end of the war.
- In 1916, Britain and France secretly agreed to divide the Turkish Empire in the Middle East between them.
- In 1917, Britain promised the Jews a homeland of their own in Palestine.

1   How accurate is it to describe the war of 1914–18 as a 'World War'?

Use the map, sources and information in this chapter to help you.

2   How important a part did the war in the Middle East play in the defeat of Germany and her allies?

... In Conclusion

- The First World War was fought in many different parts of the world.
- On the Eastern Front, Russian casualties were very high.
- The British army defeated the Turks in the Middle East.
- Germany lost her colonies in Africa and the Pacific.

PRACTISE YOUR ENQUIRY SKILLS

How far do Sources A and B (page 57) agree about casualties on the Eastern Front?

13 THE END OF THE WAR

How were the Germans defeated in 1918?

What's it all about?

When the USA entered the war in 1917, the Germans realised they must defeat Britain and France before the USA could make a real contribution to the war. The Ludendorff offensive of March 1918 almost succeeded, but by the summer, the German armies were demoralised and the Allies forced them to retreat. A ceasefire was agreed in November 1918.

THE USA ENTERS THE WAR

On 2 February 1917, Germany declared that its submarines would attempt to sink any ship heading for Britain with food or supplies. The German government hoped that this policy of unrestricted submarine warfare would starve the British into surrendering.

Almost two years earlier, German submarines had sunk a British passenger liner, the *Lusitania*, drowning 1201 of the people on board. This had greatly angered the USA because 128 American citizens died when the *Lusitania* went down. As the USA was a neutral country, her citizens should have been safe to travel without fear of attack.

When the German **U-boats** again started to sink all ships approaching Britain, huge numbers of ships went down in just a few weeks. This caused great problems in Britain – at one point the country had only six weeks supply of food left. Damage to US shipping, and the loss of American lives, contributed to the US declaration of war on 6 April 1917.

Source A

American ships have been sunk, American lives taken. I advise the US Congress to declare the recent course of the Imperial German government to be nothing less than war against the government and people of America.

Neutrality is no longer feasible or desirable. We are accepting this challenge because we know that in such a government we can never have a friend. The German government is the natural enemy of liberty. The world must be made safe for democracy.

From President Wilson's speech to US Congress, April 1917.

Source B

From the very start of the war we did everything that we could to contribute to the cause of the Allies. This had two effects. It helped the Allies in the production of goods and munitions so that they could fight the war. It also helped develop the USA's great and profitable export trade.

A US businessman writing after the war.

Glossary

U-boat: the German word for submarine is *Unterseeboot*, meaning 'under sea boat'.

1   What reasons does President Wilson (Source A) give for declaring war on Germany?

2   a) According to Source B, why did US businesses provide the Allies (Britain, France and Russia) with supplies from the start of the war?

    b) Which of these reasons do you think was the more important? Why?

RUSSIA QUITS

In early March 1917, a revolution forced the **Tsar** to abdicate. The new government was determined to continue fighting the war but soldiers started to desert, angry that there was no end to the fighting. At the beginning of November, there was a second revolution, and the **Bolsheviks** seized power. Their leader, Lenin, had promised the Russian people an end to the fighting and, in December 1917, Russia asked the Germans and Austrians for a ceasefire. In March 1918 the Treaty of Brest-Litovsk forced Russia to give up vast areas of land.

Glossary

Tsar: the Russian emperor.

Bolsheviks: Russian communists, led by Lenin.

Source C

The German response to Russian withdrawal

The German High Command now started to plan what they hoped would be a final major offensive in the West. As they no longer had to fight Russia, they would be able to move additional troops to the Western Front. General Ludendorff planned the attack for March 1918, calculating that the USA would not be ready to make a significant contribution to the fighting until later in the spring.

Source D

The situation in Russia … will make it possible to deliver a blow to the Western Front in the new year. Our general situation requires that we should strike at the earliest moment, if possible at the end of February or at the beginning of March, before the USA can throw strong forces into the scale. We must beat the British.

German military planners, 11 November 1917.

THE LUDENDORFF OFFENSIVE

On 18 March 1918, the German offensive began. A five hour bombardment was followed by an attack which forced the British to retreat. By early April, the British had been pushed back over 40 km and 70,000 British soldiers had been taken prisoner. In the end, however, the German attack failed. The Allies managed to establish, and hold, a new frontline. German casualties were high and fresh US troops were arriving all the time.

A photograph showing a Russian soldier trying to prevent two of his comrades from deserting the Eastern Front, 1917.

Source E

A tremendous roll of fire brought us to our feet. Our uncertainty was ended by the instantaneous crash, the like of which has never been heard before by land or sea, from thousands and thousands of guns roaring on a front of 30 miles. The noise was greater than anything I had ever imagined. We were stunned by literally thousands of bursting shells, and we could see that our entire front was wrapped in a sea of smoke and flame as the earth heaved and twisted under our feet.

A German soldier who witnessed the beginning of the Ludendorff offensive, 1918.

Source F

German storm troops in action during the Ludendorff offensive, 1918. These soldiers had been trained to make rapid progress by avoiding enemy strong points.

Believing victory was still possible, Ludendorff ordered further German attacks. By the end of May, German forces were only 60 km from Paris, but again the Allies managed to halt the German advance. US troops were now fighting alongside the Allies. In June, an additional 275,000 US soldiers landed in France. When the German army tried a final attack on the Marne in July, the Allies counter-attacked. Their morale broken, the German army was forced to retreat.

Why was German morale broken?

- Through the spring and early summer, the German army suffered high casualties while Allied forces were strengthened by increasing numbers of US troops.

- For almost four years, the British had been blockading German ports, making it difficult to import food and other necessities. By 1918, there were acute food shortages in Germany; even the army was hungry (there were rumours that German troops were stopping to steal food from farms).

Source G

In the summer of 1918, Berlin ran out of potatoes, while thousands of soldiers on leave told their families that the war could not be won. Their loyalty to the Kaiser's government was at an end. Many of these infantrymen never made it back to their units. They 'unofficially' extended their leave until the war was over.

From a recent history of the First World War.

Source H

The strain of the Ludendorff offensive on the German army was very great, and total German casualties for this period amounted to nearly 1 million men including 125,000 dead and 100,000 missing. There was also a steep decline in morale. German soldiers, short of supplies, plundered enemy supplies and alcohol where possible, while many German soldiers deserted. Then in June and July, the influenza epidemic hit the German army with more than half a million cases.

From *World War I: a history,* (1998), edited by Hew Strachan.

Source I

There is no course open to us but to fight it out! Every position must be held to the last man. With our backs to the wall, and believing in the justice of our cause, each one of us must fight on to the end. The safety of our homes and the freedom of mankind depend on the conduct of each one of us.

Field Marshal Haig's message to the troops, April 1918

> 1 Explain why the Russian withdrawal from the First World War was so important for Germany.
>
> 2 Why did the Ludendorff offensive fail?

8 AUGUST 1918 – THE 'BLACK DAY' OF THE GERMAN ARMY

On 8 August 1918 the Allies launched a massive attack on the Somme, near the town of Amiens in France. Bogus radio signals were used to disguise troop movements and fighter planes were used to keep enemy spotter planes away, so the Germans were taken by surprise.

■ There was no bombardment before the attack to alert the Germans.

■ At 4 am a massive force attacked under the cover of a creeping barrage provided by over 2000 guns and howitzers.

■ The Allies advanced, protected by accurate artillery fire, which eliminated enemy guns and machine-gun posts.

■ Over 500 tanks lumbered forward, while Allied planes **strafed** German troops as they retreated.

■ Radio was used to maintain contact between the air and land forces. By the end of the day, demoralised German soldiers were starting to surrender in large numbers. Many of them had simply had enough.

Glossary

strafe: to attack ground troops with machine-gun fire from low-flying aeroplanes.

blackleg: a soldier who refused to cooperate with those who wanted to surrender.

Source J

8 August 1918 was the black day of the German army. I summoned divisional commanders and officers from the line to discuss events with them in detail. I was told of deeds of glorious valour but also of behaviour which I openly confess, I should not have thought possible in the German army. Whole bodies of our men had surrendered to single troopers. Retiring troops, meeting a fresh division going bravely into action, had shouted out things like '**Blackleg**' and 'You're prolonging the war'.

General Ludendorff.

Source K

The German defenders at Amiens had no response to the Allied onslaught. From this point onward, the result of the war was never in doubt. Amiens demonstrated the extent of the military revolution that occurred on the Western Front between 1914 and 1918. It was a modern battle.

A historian writing in 2002.

THE USE OF TANKS ON 8 AUGUST 1918

- 534 tanks went into action.
- By the following day, there were only 145 in working order.
- On 12 August, after just four days of fighting, only six tanks were fit for use in action.

THE FINAL STAGES OF THE FIRST WORLD WAR

Although fighting continued in France and Belgium, developments elsewhere were bringing the war to an end.

- On 29 September, Bulgaria, Germany's ally, surrendered.
- On 29 October, German sailors went on strike. There were strikes and riots elsewhere in Germany.
- On 30 October, Turkey surrendered.
- In November, Austria-Hungary surrendered.
- On 9 November, the Kaiser fled to Holland. The new German government asked the Allies for a ceasefire.
- 11 November: at 11 am the fighting ended. The ceasefire, or armistice, had begun.

···▸ Activity

There are a number of reasons why Germany and her allies lost the war. These include:

- US involvement in the war
- the failure of the Ludendorff offensive
- the long-term effects of the Allied naval blockade of Germany
- the part played by new technology in breaking the stalemate
- the defeat of Germany's allies.

1 Working in groups of three or four, create a mind map showing the main reasons why Germany was defeated. At this stage your diagram will look like the one on page 5.

2 Taking each of the main reasons in turn, identify several ways in which it contributed to the defeat of Germany and her allies. Add these to your diagram so that you show all of the ways in which each reason contributed to the defeat of Germany. For instance, US involvement meant that many more soldiers were available to fight on the Western Front. Show that this was a result of US involvement in the war. What else did the USA contribute to the War? In what other ways did US involvement contribute to the defeat of Germany?

3 Discuss your mind map with another group in your class.

⋯⋰ *Activity*

4   Use your mind map to help answer the following question:

How important a part did US involvement in the First World War play in the defeat of Germany?

To answer this question, you should write a short essay of several paragraphs.

■   Your essay should have an introduction and a conclusion.

■   Remember to consider other possible reasons why Germany was defeated, as well as the part played by US involvement.

... IN CONCLUSION

⋯⋰ ■   In April 1917, the USA declared war on Germany.

■   Russia withdrew from the First World War in December 1917.

■   In March 1918, the Ludendorff offensive forced the Allies to retreat.

■   Germany's will to fight weakened in the summer of 1918.

■   In August, the Allies launched a very successful offensive on the Somme.

■   By October 1918, Germany's allies were surrendering.

■   On 11 November 1918, an armistice was signed and the fighting ended.

PRACTISE YOUR ENQUIRY SKILLS

1   How useful is Source A (page 59) as evidence of US attitudes towards the declaration of war?

2   How far do Sources G and H (page 61) agree about morale in the German army in the summer of 1918?

3   Look at Source J (page 62). What was General Ludendorff's attitude towards the events of 8 August 1918?

THE HOME FRONT IN BRITAIN: GOVERNING A COUNTRY AT WAR

How did the government change life in Britain during the First World War?

What's it all about?

The First World War had a significant impact on life in Britain.
The government intervened more in people's lives and reduced individual freedom. Although huge numbers of men volunteered for the army, conscription was introduced in 1916 and food shortages eventually led to rationing.

BUSINESS AS USUAL?

When the First World War started in August 1914, most people believed that life in Britain would not be affected much. Shopkeepers and traders called for 'Business as Usual', and the slogan received considerable publicity when the London store Harrods used it in an advertising campaign.

The government, too, wanted business to continue normally, but the demands of organising such a huge war effort meant that government control over people's lives increased. The government also had to take responsibility for things that had previously been left to private individuals and businesses.

The Defence of the Realm Act 1914

On 8 August 1914, a very important new law was passed. The Defence of the Realm Act (DORA) allowed the government to introduce whatever restrictions proved necessary to protect the country during the war. Some of these new regulations were introduced immediately. Others were added during the course of the war.

DORA gave the government far more control over people's lives than would have been considered acceptable during peacetime. People were forbidden to:

- take photos of military bases
- attempt to get information about military matters
- own homing pigeons without permission
- fly flags or use other signalling equipment
- use invisible ink when writing abroad
- give bread to animals or poultry
- ring church bells
- spread false rumours.

In addition, the following new regulations were introduced:

- censorship of newspapers was permitted
- pub opening hours were limited
- beer was watered down so that the alcohol content was reduced
- British Summer Time (BST) was introduced, to give more daylight working hours
- Guy Fawkes' night bonfires were banned.

MANAGING WEAPONS PRODUCTION

At first, the British economy could not meet the production demands for **munitions** created by the First World War.

Source A

One mile of trench required 900 miles of barbed wire, 6 million sandbags, 1 million cubic feet of timber and 360,000 square feet of corrugated iron.

A modern historian writing in 1996.

Source B

The infantry did splendidly, but the conditions were too hard. The lack of an unlimited supply of high explosives was a fatal bar to our success.

Extract from *The Times* newspaper, 14 May 1915.

Glossary

munitions: weapons, particularly shells and explosives.

TUC: Trades Union Congress, the main organisation representing workers.

In May 1915, *The Times* newspaper revealed that there was a serious shortage of shells that was affecting the army's ability to fight, and endangering soldiers' lives. The story was taken up by the *Daily Mail*. Eventually, the prime minister, Herbert Henry Asquith, was forced to recognise that 'business as usual' was not working. He set up a new government department, the Ministry of Munitions, to oversee wartime production. In July, a new Act of Parliament gave David Lloyd George, the government minister in charge of the new ministry, the power to do whatever was necessary to increase the production of munitions.

Lloyd George had greater powers than any minister had ever had in peacetime. He could:

- take over existing factories and tell them what to produce
- set up new government-run factories
- take over the land needed for building new factories
- control the supplies of coal needed to provide fuel
- control the railways needed to transport munitions.

Source C

DELIVERING THE GOODS.

A *Punch* cartoon of 1915, showing David Lloyd George 'Delivering the Goods'.

Shortly after the war started, the **TUC** agreed to cooperate with the government. Strikes would be avoided and workers would help with the war effort. During the war, strikes were less frequent than they had been in the years immediately before the outbreak of war, but the fear of strike action remained a problem for the government. One of the areas which caused the government most concern was Clydeside in the west of Scotland. There were a number of reasons why the workers on the Clyde felt unfairly treated:

- unskilled workers were brought in to work alongside skilled workers, who objected to this 'dilution' of skilled labour
- new ways of working were introduced which made skilled work less important.

These developments seemed to threaten the jobs of skilled workers. Local shop stewards set up the Clyde Workers Committee and demanded more worker control over industry. In 1916, the government arrested the leaders and imprisoned them or deported them to Edinburgh. Deportees had to sign an undertaking not to engage in industrial unrest (see Source D).

Source D

I (name and address) hereby undertake that if I am permitted by the military authorities to reside in or near Glasgow, I will, while there, remain at work at my trade, provided that suitable work is available, and will, during the continuance of the war, take no part, directly or indirectly, in any stoppage of work or in any action designed to secure a stoppage, or in any other action which is likely in any way to delay or interfere in the manufacture or supply of munitions, or any other work required for the successful prosecution of the war. I undertake further that should I have any grievances which I consider to require redress, I will submit them to be dealt with through the usual constitutional channels by the recognised trade union to which I belong.

9/10 August 1916

Undertaking to be signed by the Clyde deportees.

RECRUITMENT

Government propaganda: 'Is your best boy wearing khaki?'

One of the first things that the government had to do was to recruit thousands of young men into the army. The Parliamentary Recruiting Committee was set up by a group of MPs to mastermind propaganda posters to encourage young men to join up. One early poster asked women: 'Is your **best boy** wearing khaki? If not, don't you think he should be?'

Glossary

best boy: boyfriend.

Source E

LINE UP, BOYS!

ENLIST TO-DAY.

A Scottish recruiting poster.

1 Choose five different regulations introduced under DORA. Explain how each measure was supposed to increase national security during the First World War.

2 Explain why the government increased its control over the economy during the war. Use Sources A and B in your answer.

3 Look at Source C.

a) What is the significance of the speed with which the rider is driving the cart forward?

b) Why are the two horses called 'Labour' and 'Capital'?

4 Read Source D. Why did the government remove some of the Clyde Workers Committee leaders from Glasgow?

Attitudes towards recruitment

Many people helped in the recruitment campaign. Women gave white feathers – a symbol of cowardice – to young men who had not joined up; employers urged their workers to enlist. The entire Heart of Midlothian football team volunteered to serve, and many of the team's supporters followed their example.

Source F

Once war broke out, the situation at home became awful, because people did not like to see men or lads of army age walking about in civilian clothing, or not in uniform of some sort. Women were the worst. They would come up to you in the street and give you a white feather, or stick it in the lapel of your coat ... they meant you were a coward and that you should be in the army doing your bit for king and country.

William Brooks, who joined the army in 1915.

Source G

The Nestle Company publicly announced that it expected all single male employees between eighteen and 30 to volunteer. A firm of stockbrokers in London told its staff, 'The firm expects that all unmarried staff under 35 years of age will join Earl Kitchener's army at once.'

A modern historian writing in 1996.

Pals' Battalions

Within days of the declaration of war, the War Ministry came up with an idea to encourage recruitment. Men from the same workplace, or town, could join the same battalion in the army if they joined up together. These battalions were known as Pals' battalions. By December 1914, over 1700 men from the Glasgow Corporation Tramways had volunteered for the Highland Light Infantry Glasgow Tramways Battalion. 285 of these volunteers died in the first few days of fighting in the Somme in 1916.

Conscription

Over 2.5 million men volunteered for the army between August 1914 and December 1915. By then, however, the numbers of volunteers were falling and, with the high casualty figures on the Western Front, the government decided to introduce conscription.

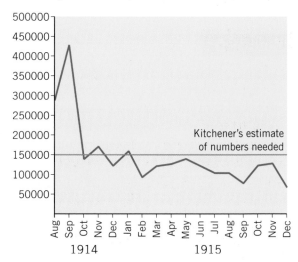

Voluntary recruitment for the army in Britain, August 1914 to December 1915.

The Military Service Act 1916 introduced compulsory military service, although men could apply for exemption on grounds of occupation or religious and moral belief. At first, the Act only applied to unmarried men aged 18 to 41, but in May 1916, it was extended to include married men.

1   Describe some of the ways in which men were persuaded to enlist.

2   Explain why the government introduced conscription in January 1916.

Conscientious objectors

In total, there were over 16,000 conscientious objectors – men who objected to fighting on either moral or religious grounds – during the First World War. Many of those who applied for exemption from fighting were socialists or Quakers.

The vast majority of conscientious objectors were prepared to accept non-combatant military duties such as working as stretcher bearers and ambulance men. Those who refused to have anything to do with the war effort were imprisoned.

Source H

There were some shameful cases of sadistic treatment. One inmate of Camberwell Prison, told he would be executed, was slowly taken through the motions of an actual execution, to the point of the gun being loaded and pointed at him. Inmates were force-fed, tied into straight jackets, beaten, kept in filthy cells, fed on bread and water and often tortured.

A modern historian describes the treatment of some conscientious objectors during the First World War.

FOOD SHORTAGES

U-boat attacks

As Britain imported a large amount of raw materials and food from overseas, German submarines threatened Britain's ability to keep on fighting the war.

U-boats were first used to attack merchant ships in 1915. However, this naval campaign was called off later that year after pressure from the USA following the sinking of the *Lusitania* (see page 59). In October 1916, the Germans started to attack merchant shipping again, and the situation became very serious when unrestricted submarine warfare began in February 1917. In April 1917, over 500,000 tons of shipping were sunk, and Britain was left with only six weeks supply of wheat.

The Ministry of Food

Until the end of 1917, the government encouraged people to reduce food consumption voluntarily. A Ministry of Food was established but, at first, it was not very effective. Meatless days were organised and the throwing of rice at weddings was forbidden; there were even restrictions on what kind of food could be served in tea-shops! At the same time, all available land was turned over to allotments so people could grow more food. Because supplies of wheat were running low, bread also contained potato and bean flour; margarine replaced butter. Posters drew attention to the problems created by wasting food; at the cinema, short propaganda films encouraged people to 'do their bit' and economise.

Source I

A government poster aimed at women, March 1917.

At the same time, the government organised merchant shipping into convoys, protected by the navy, which reduced U-boat damage.

The introduction of rationing

Despite the voluntary campaign to reduce consumption, food shortages continued and prices rose. In the autumn of 1917, the government introduced subsidies for bread and potatoes to prevent prices rising further. In December, sugar rationing was introduced, followed in the summer of 1918 by butter, margarine, tea, cooking fat, meat, bacon, ham and jam.

Rationing solved the problems of shortages and rising prices. Although the rich still ate much better than the poor, nobody starved and some people actually ate better because they had a more balanced diet.

Source J

Figures indicate that the families of unskilled workmen were slightly better fed by 1918, in spite of the rise in the price of food. From London, it is officially reported, after inspection of all children entering school, that 'the percentage of children found in a poorly nourished condition is considerably less than half the percentage of 1913'.

From a government report, published in 1918.

1   How did the British government deal with the food shortages created by the U-boat threat?

... In Conclusion

- The Defence of the Realm Act (DORA) increased government control over people's lives and the economy.
- Over 2.5 million men volunteered for the army in 1914–15.
- The numbers of volunteers finally started to decline and conscription was introduced in 1916.
- Food shortages led to rationing at the end of 1917.

PRACTISE YOUR ENQUIRY SKILLS

1   How valuable is Source C (page 66) as evidence of changes that took place in the British economy during the war?

2   What does Source H (page 69) reveal about some people's attitudes towards conscientious objectors during the First World War?

3   How fully does Source J (above) describe the effects of the war on people's standard of living? Use evidence from the source and your own knowledge to answer this question.

15 THE HOME FRONT IN BRITAIN: THE PEOPLE AT WAR

How did civilians' lives change during the First World War?

What's it all about?

Women made an important contribution to the war effort and worked in a variety of different jobs. Many people faced problems such as food and fuel shortages, as well as the anxieties and grief caused by war. Propaganda was used to keep up morale and to persuade people that their efforts were worthwhile.

HOW DID WOMEN'S LIVES CHANGE?

When war broke out in 1914, people of all social classes were affected. For women, in particular, the First World War brought many changes. Although many women worked outside the home by 1914, for others, the war brought new independence and new opportunities.

The changes in women's lives did not come suddenly. When an Edinburgh doctor, Elsie Inglis, contacted the War Office in 1914 and asked what she could do to help, she was told: 'My good lady, go home and sit still.' But as more and more men enlisted, women were needed to fill the jobs they left behind to help keep the country running.

Campaigning for the right to work

Many women had been campaigning for the right to vote in the years before the war. With the outbreak of war, women instead turned their efforts to campaigning for the right to be part of the war effort. The leaders of the movements campaigning for votes for women, Emily Pankhurst and Millicent Fawcett, organised a massive demonstration on 15 July 1915. Banners carried the words, 'We demand the right to work' and 'Shells made by a wife may save a husband's life'.

What sort of work did women do?

By the end of the war there were over 7 million women in employment, about 25 per cent more than had been working in 1914.

- Many working-class women were employed in the munitions industry – one government minister reckoned that women were producing about 80 per cent of all shells and weapons by 1918.

- Other women joined the Women's Land Army and worked in agriculture.

- From 1916 onwards, women could join the Women's Royal Naval Service (WRNS) where clerical and support jobs, previously done by men, were now handed over to women. The popularity of the WRNS led to the creation of the Women's Auxiliary Army Corps (WAAC) the following year, and the Women's Royal Air Force (WRAF) in 1918.

- Middle-class women were more likely to work as nurses with the Voluntary Aid Detachment (VAD) established by the Red Cross in 1909 – by the end of the war there were over 90,000 people involved in VAD work.

- Middle-class women also worked as factory supervisors, with responsibility for the welfare of women workers, or found employment in either local or national government.

- Many women took responsibility for running the family business while male family members fought in the war.

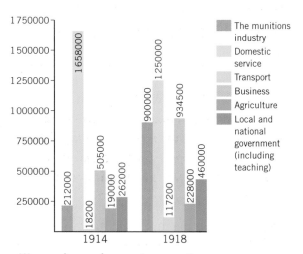

Women in employment, 1914–18.

1 Using the graph and information on pages 71–3, describe some of the work done by women during the First World War.

2 Look at the graph. In which area of employment was there the biggest percentage increase? How do you explain this change?

3 In which area of employment did numbers decline? How do you explain this?

The Munitionettes

When the Ministry of Munitions was set up in 1915, the government needed to recruit women workers. Although advertisements and posters tried to create a positive image of the work, many women were reluctant to work in munitions. Even at the end of the war, there were more women working as servants than there were working in munitions.

Source A

A government poster of 1915.

Working in munitions was unhealthy and the TNT used in the explosives often turned skin yellow, earning the women the nickname 'canaries'. Over 100 women are known to have died from TNT poisoning during the First World War. In addition to being dangerous, munitions work was not well paid. Women usually earned less than men doing the same job: on average, they received about 60 per cent of an average male worker's wage.

Source B

The girls turn yellow and then many of them get horrible rashes, and their faces swell up so that they are for a day or two quite blind, and most repulsive objects. Nevertheless, when they are cured, they go back, and run the risk of getting ill again.

A canteen worker recalls the effects of working in a munitions factory during the First World War.

The Women's Land Army

The government also established the Women's Land Army to recruit women from the towns to go and work on farms. Despite a persuasive poster campaign, the Women's Land Army was never very large and many farmers treated the women who joined with suspicion. The work was very hard and the hours were long, so many women preferred factory work. In fact, most of the additional workforce needed on farms came from local women, rather than the towns.

Source C

A recruitment poster for the Women's Land Army.

> Study Sources A and C carefully.
>
> Explain how government posters tried to make war work attractive to women.

Did the war change the status of women?

At the time, many people claimed that the war had permanently changed women's position in society. Today, historians are more sceptical. The government had agreed with the trade unions that when the war ended returning male workers could have their jobs back, and so many women lost their jobs in 1918. By 1921, there were slightly fewer women in employment than there were in 1911.

HOW MUCH WERE THE LIVES OF BRITISH PEOPLE AFFECTED BY THE WAR?

Shortages and strikes

The war had a major impact on people's lives. By 1917, shortages of food and fuel led to lengthy queues, a problem which was only solved when rationing was introduced (see page 70).

Source D

The usual potato and coal scenes took place yesterday. In South London, trolleymen with coals were besieged by people who had brought all types of vehicles, including prams, wheelbarrows, go-carts and trucks, while others had sacks, baskets and boxes. The would-be purchasers assembled soon after 7 am in the morning and the queue of waiting women and children extended to a great length within an hour.

At Wrexham, a big farm wagon laden with potatoes was brought into the square. The wagon was surrounded by hundreds of clamouring people, chiefly women, who scrambled onto the vehicle in their eagerness to buy. Several women fainted in the struggle and the police were sent to restore order.

From the *Observer* newspaper, October 1917.

In Glasgow in 1916, when munitions workers moved into the area, there were rent increases as landlords tried to exploit the sudden demand for housing. Local women played a significant part in organising a successful rent strike which eventually forced the government to fix rents for the rest of the war.

Zeppelin raids and child labour

The Zeppelin raids also had an impact. Although the bombs dropped by Zeppelin airships did not do anything like as much damage as bombing during the Second World War, the raids caused considerable panic and alarm. A Zeppelin attack on Edinburgh, in April 1916, killed thirteen people and caused extensive damage.

Children, too, were affected by the war. Except in some munitions factories, there were few nurseries for mothers with young children. Although the school leaving age was officially fourteen, over half a million children under that age had some kind of job during the war, and the strict rules regarding child workers were often disregarded.

Receiving news from the front

For families throughout Britain, there was the constant fear of a telegram or letter bringing bad news. Nearly every family in the land was affected in some way by the slaughter that was taking place on the Western Front and elsewhere. War did not discriminate between rich and poor when claiming lives. The prime minister's son was killed in action during the Battle of the Somme. Thousands of others, long since forgotten, also died: only the war memorials in Britain and France record their names.

Glossary

Hun: a barbarian.

Regret to inform you that Lieut. R. A. Leighton 7th Worcesters died of wounds December 23rd. Lord Kitchener sends his sympathy.

A telegram sent to inform a family about the death of a soldier.

PROPAGANDA AND THE WAR EFFORT

The government persuaded people to support the war in a number of different ways. In the first year of the war alone, 110 different posters were produced, urging people to join the army or help the war effort at home. By 1917, the government had set up a Department of Information; in 1918, Lord Beaverbrook, who owned the *Daily Express* newspaper, was appointed Minister of Information.

Anti-German propaganda

British wartime propaganda portrayed German people as '**Huns**', and German civilisation and culture were mocked. This theme was used throughout the war to convince British people that they were fighting on the side of truth and justice. In reality, truth was often distorted; sometimes facts were invented to present the Germans in a bad light.

Source F

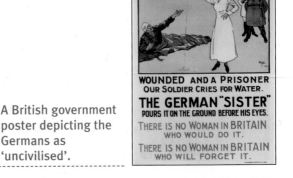

RED CROSS or IRON CROSS?

WOUNDED AND A PRISONER
OUR SOLDIER CRIES FOR WATER.
THE GERMAN "SISTER"
POURS IT ON THE GROUND BEFORE HIS EYES.
THERE IS NO WOMAN IN BRITAIN
WHO WOULD DO IT.
THERE IS NO WOMAN IN BRITAIN
WHO WILL FORGET IT.

A British government poster depicting the Germans as 'uncivilised'.

Source G

The front page of a children's comic, 1914.

Source H

The most famous propaganda achievement of the war was the story that the Germans were converting the bodies of dead soldiers into lubricating oils, pig food and manure. The story first appeared in *The Times* but then a Department of Information leaflet, headed 'A Corpse Conversion Factory', spread the story. It was only in 1925 that it was admitted in the House of Commons that the story had been invented.

A modern historian, 1991.

1   How important a part did anti-German propaganda play in persuading people to support the war?

·····› Activity

Some historians claim that the First World War changed life in Britain considerably. Others claim that most of the changes were only temporary.

1   Copy the table below into your notes.

Aspect of life changed by the war	Political	Economic	Social	Did the change last?

a)   Look through Chapters 13 and 14 and find examples of changes that took place during the First World War. Enter the information into the table.

b)   Try to find out whether each of the changes you identified lasted after the end of the First World War.

2   *'The First World War changed life in Britain forever.'*

How far do you agree with this statement? Use the evidence you have collected to reach a balanced conclusion.

... IN CONCLUSION

····› During the First World War:
- women played an important part on the Home Front
- the people of Britain had to cope with a number of difficulties
- loss and bereavement affected almost every family in the country
- wartime propaganda may have influenced how people thought.

PRACTISE YOUR ENQUIRY SKILLS

Source I

> When myths are stripped away, this period no longer seems a golden age of women's emancipation. Women were primarily seen as cheap, easily exploitable labour, useful in a crisis but possessing very little value in their own right.

A modern historian, Gerard De Groot, writing in 1996.

1   Discuss the attitude of the historian in Source I towards the impact the First World War had on changing the status of women.

2   How fully does Source D (page 73) describe the hardships women faced during the First World War?

THE HOME FRONT IN GERMANY

How were German civilians affected by the First World War?

What's it all about?

People in Germany faced severe hardship as a result of the war. The British blockade of German ports created shortages and there was not enough food to go round. By the end of the war, many people were dying of starvation. Women in Germany made an important contribution to the war effort.

THE BRITISH NAVAL BLOCKADE OF GERMANY

From the beginning of the war, Britain used her fleet to stop Germany importing goods and food. Before the war, Germany had imported almost half of all the raw materials she needed, so the blockade by the navy to prevent shipping reaching Germany created acute shortages.

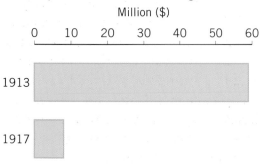

Germany's overseas trade shown in millions of dollars, 1913–17.

As a result of the blockade:

- industry ran out of rubber
- farmers did not have enough fertilisers to grow their crops
- various metals were in short supply

- there was a shortage of coal and, as this was needed to generate gas and electricity, there were lengthy power cuts
- there was a shortage of cotton for clothing; leather was so scarce that the leather belts used to drive machinery in factories were replaced with cotton ones and many people had to wear wooden shoes.

Although the German government worked hard to develop 'substitute' products, such as clothing made from specially processed paper, synthetic rubber and artificial fertilisers, many of these substitutes were expensive to manufacture and did not work well.

Source A

A vest made from processed paper in Germany during the First World War.

Source B

In addition to other hardships, the German public is threatened this winter with an almost complete lack of lights of every description: electric light, gas, lamp oil and candles. The lack of soap and washing powder makes personal cleanliness impossible and helps the spread of disease. Medicines are difficult to obtain. Many of the women have hardly any clothing and are going about in a thin blouse and skirt, bare legged with wooden shoes.

A British Foreign Office report, 1918.

Source C

A poster produced in Germany during the First World War, which reads 'There is aluminum, copper, brass, nickel, tin in the country. Hand it over – the army needs it!'

> What effects did the Allied blockade have on the German economy?

FOOD SHORTAGES AND THE 'TURNIP WINTER'

Only about 20 per cent of Germany's food was imported before the war and so on its own the British naval blockade did not greatly reduce the amount of food available. However, it did cut off supplies of fertilisers and this had a serious effect on food production.

To make matters worse, pig farmers, who were no longer able to import animal feed, started to use potatoes and grain to feed their animals. As this was using up valuable food supplies, the government ordered a mass slaughter of pigs in the spring of 1915. In the long run, this created a meat shortage that pushed meat prices up until the government was forced to introduce meat rationing.

Poor harvests made problems worse. Bread rationing was introduced in February 1915 and 'war bread', made with up to 30 per cent potato flour, replaced ordinary bread. Potatoes were also in short supply and things got so bad that in the winter of 1916–17 many people in the towns were forced to eat turnips instead. The daily calorie intake that winter was around 1100 calories – about half what an adult needs. People were lucky if they managed to get hold of one egg a fortnight.

Source D

That dreadful winter of 1916–17 we ate five or six hundredweight of turnips. In the morning we had turnip soup, at midday we ate turnip cutlets, in the evening we had turnip cakes. All the same, we were a lot better off than hundreds of thousands of others.

From the memoirs of Walter Koch, a local government official.

Source E

Substitute foods were produced to make up for shortages during the war. This claims to be nourishing food made with potato and synthetic strawberry flavouring. It contains neither milk nor egg!

Chemical industry

26 749

208 877

Engineering works

74 642

493 374

Numbers of women working in the German chemical industry and engineering works, 1913–18.

Over 750,000 people died from starvation or malnutrition in Germany during the First World War, and a further 150,000, weakened by lack of food, died in the flu epidemic of 1918. Historians do not agree whether these deaths were caused by the Allied naval blockade or by poor harvests and inefficient distribution of food.

THE WAR EFFORT ON THE HOME FRONT

As in Britain, women in Germany took on jobs previously done by men. Many women worked twelve-hour shifts in industry, while others tended allotments in towns. As food shortages grew more severe, town workers often travelled by train into the countryside at weekends, desperately hoping to buy extra food on the 'black market'.

In August 1916, all men aged between seventeen and 60 who were not in the army were required to do war work. The aim was to increase the production of munitions, machine guns and artillery. This meant that that there were fewer people working on the land and this made the food shortages worse.

Did propaganda persuade people to support the war?

As in other countries, propaganda aimed to present a positive image of the war. While British posters criticised the uncivilised 'Hun' (see page 74), German posters represented Germany as the civilised country and portrayed Britain and France in an unfavourable way. Poster campaigns also persuaded people to subscribe to war loans, which were an important way of financing the war.

At the start of the war, there were far fewer cinemas in Germany than there were in Britain, but by 1917, German newsreels were becoming increasingly popular. The German army had its own film unit, combining a popular form of entertainment with patriotism.

'A mixture of compulsion and persuasion.'
How well does this describe the German war effort?

DID THE GERMAN PEOPLE SUPPORT THE WAR BY 1918?

By 1918, many Germans were war-weary. Even though the fighting on the Eastern Front had ended, the Ludendorff offensive (see pages 60–1) meant that the casualty rate remained high.

Because the government printed paper money to help pay for the war, the German currency (the mark) fell in value. By 1918, it was worth about 25 per cent of what it had been worth in 1914. Meanwhile, the cost of living continued to rise. As poverty and hardship increased, there were demonstrations in some German cities. Many workers wanted an end to the war and a government that would end the differences between rich and poor. Wealthy Germans realised that, if the war continued, such discontent could lead to a revolution like the communist takeover in Russia (see page 60), which would end their prosperity forever.

On 9 November 1918, Germany was declared a Republic and the Kaiser fled to Holland. Two days later, the new government accepted the Allies terms for an armistice.

After the war, the Allied naval blockade of Germany continued and food shortages remained. This photo was taken in Berlin, probably in January 1919. It shows people cutting up a dead horse in the street so that they can eat the meat.

⋯⋗ Activity

Organise a class debate on the motion:

'Germany lost the First World War on the Home Front, not the Western Front.'

■ To prepare for the debate, first list all the evidence that supports the motion.

■ Then make a second list of all of the evidence which suggests this view is not accurate.

■ Be ready to speak either *for* or *against* the motion.

Keep a record of your debate. You could publish a summary of your arguments on your school's web pages or Intranet.

... IN CONCLUSION

- The British naval blockade of Germany created severe shortages.
- Many Germans died of starvation or malnutrition during the war.
- Women, young people and older men contributed to the war effort on the Home Front.
- The German government used propaganda to persuade people to support the war effort.
- By 1918, many Germans sought an end to the war.

PRACTISE YOUR ENQUIRY SKILLS

Source H

By 1916, the Germans had already started the story that their food shortage was due to the British 'hunger blockade'. Yet Germany had not imported food before the war. The truth is that the Germans starved themselves. They took millions of men from the land for the armies. High prices encouraged the peasants to send their pigs and cattle to market. Then supplies ran short. 1916 saw a bad harvest, followed by a bitter winter. Turnips became the staple diet.

A historian writing in 1963.

Source I

We have got through a queer week – the worst week the German people has had to face. No coal, electric light turned off, the gas turned down, and practically no food. There seem to be no more potatoes. Each of us has been given half a pound of what they call potato-*flocken*. I know no English word for it. They seem to be dried potato peelings – you have to soak them overnight and then rub them through a sieve. We had that half-pound, five pounds of turnips, three and a half pounds of bread, and that was all.

  I went the rounds of the restaurants and I managed to get some cabbage or a tiny piece of chicken, or edible toadstools, and I bought some tinned fish, but it passes my understanding to know how the poor are managing.

A letter written by an Australian woman living in Germany, February 1917.

Source J

We have no meat. Potatoes cannot be delivered because we are short of 4000 trucks a day. Fat is unobtainable. The shortage is so great that it is a mystery to me what the people of Berlin live on. The workers say, 'Better a horrible end than an endless horror.'

A member of the German government, 1918.

1   Discuss the attitude of the author in Source H towards the causes of the food shortages in Germany during the First World War.

2   How far do Sources I and J agree about the hardships of life in Berlin during the last two years of the First World War?

3   How fully does Source D (page 79) describe conditions in Germany during the 'Turnip Winter' of 1916–17?

17 PEACEMAKING, 1919

How fair was the peace settlement after the First World War?

What's it all about?

The terms of the peace settlement after the First World War were drawn up without consulting Germany and her allies. Some aspects of the settlement were very harsh and many Germans felt bitter and resentful about the treaty.

THE PARIS PEACE CONFERENCE

Although an armistice had been signed on 11 November 1918, the terms of a permanent peace settlement still had to be agreed. In January 1919, just two months after the ceasefire, representatives of 32 countries met at Versailles, outside Paris, to draw up a peace settlement with the defeated nations. Germany and her allies were excluded from discussions about the terms of the peace treaty.

The peace conference at Versailles was dominated by the leaders of the three most powerful nations, otherwise known as the 'Big Three':

- the President of the USA, Woodrow Wilson
- the British prime minister, David Lloyd George
- the French prime minister, Georges Clemenceau.

What did the Allies want from the peace settlement?

All the representatives at Versailles wanted to agree peace terms as soon as possible.

The British naval blockade of German ports continued in case Germany tried to start the war again and as a result the German people were starving. There were also severe problems in Britain and France and the leaders of both countries wanted to return home to tackle these difficulties.

It was not going to be easy to draw up a satisfactory peace treaty. Each of the main leaders wanted something different (see pages 84–85). In the final weeks of the war, the Austro-Hungarian Empire had fallen apart and there were now new countries such as Czechoslovakia, Hungary and Poland to be taken into consideration.

In addition, the Bolshevik revolution in Russia (see page 60) had frightened many European governments, which feared that communism might spread. In January 1919, communists in Germany had tried to overthrow the new German Republic. Many people thought that, if the hardships of poverty and uncertainty continued after the war, communism might become a popular alternative and more governments could be overthrown. Such concerns increased the pressure to draw up a peace settlement quickly.

···⫶ *Activity*

Historians have been very critical of the process of peacemaking in 1919. They have identified a number of ways in which the Paris Peace Conference was flawed. At the time, however, these danger signs were ignored.

a) Working in pairs, read through the text about the Paris Peace Conference, and the information about the 'Big Three' on pages 84–85.

b) Identify at least six different 'danger signs' and explain why each one created a problem. The first one has been done for you:

Danger sign	Reason why this created problems
The peacemakers met only two months after the end of the war.	Anti-German feelings were still running high.

The terms of the peace settlement

On 8 May 1919, representatives of the German government were presented with the terms of the Treaty of Versailles. There were to be no negotiations: if they did not accept the terms, the war would start again. In the eyes of the Germans, it was a 'dictated' peace – they had had no say as to its terms.

On 28 June 1919, exactly five years after the assassination of Archduke Franz Ferdinand at Sarajevo, two German delegates signed the Treaty of Versailles in the Hall of Mirrors at Versailles. This was an especially humiliating moment because, almost 50 years earlier, the German Empire had been proclaimed (see page 7) in the very same Hall of Mirrors. Separate peace treaties were also signed with Germany's allies – Austria, Hungary, Bulgaria and Turkey.

THE 'BIG THREE' AT THE PARIS PEACE CONFERENCE

Source A

The 'Big Three' at the Paris Peace Conference. The British prime minister, Lloyd George, is on the right; President Wilson, is in the centre and the French prime minister, Clemenceau, stands next to him on the left.

Woodrow Wilson, President of the USA

Before entering politics, Wilson had been a university professor. In January 1918, he had drawn up a set of proposals for a future peace settlement. He hoped that these 'Fourteen Points' would provide 'a just and stable peace' that would prevent war in the future.

Wilson did not want the defeated countries to be humiliated. An important aim of the Fourteen Points was that different national groups in Europe should be allowed to establish independent nations of their own. This principle was known as 'self-determination'. Another of the Fourteen Points called for international disarmament. The last of Wilson's Fourteen Points proposed the setting up of a League of Nations, to act as an international peacekeeper by helping to settle future problems.

When the Germans accepted the armistice in 1918, they believed that the peace settlement would be based on Wilson's Fourteen Points. By 1919, however, Wilson had accepted that the Germans would have to pay some of the costs of the war.

Georges Clemenceau, Prime Minister of France

Clemenceau, nicknamed 'the Tiger', was 78 years old when the Paris Peace Conference began. He had not forgotten the humiliating defeat Germany had inflicted on France during the Franco-Prussian War of 1870–1 (see page 7), and now demanded the return of Alsace and Lorraine to France. He also wanted to make sure that Germany was forced to pay all the costs of the damage done to France during the war. He hoped this would weaken Germany so much that she would never be able to threaten France again.

Clemenceau's main aim at the Paris Peace Conference was to safeguard France against future attack, so he insisted on the **disarmament** of Germany. He also demanded that the German Rhineland should be transferred to France to prevent a German attack in the future.

Glossary

disarmament: the giving up of a country's military and weapons.

David Lloyd George, Prime Minister of Britain

Lloyd George believed that Germany should not be treated too harshly as this would only lead to more problems in the future. However, most British people were influenced by newspaper headlines, such as 'Make Germany Pay' and 'Hang the Kaiser', and Lloyd George was under pressure from the British government to make sure that Germany was punished for her part in the war.

Although Lloyd George was opposed to allowing the French to take the Rhineland from Germany, he wanted to make sure that Germany's navy was handed over to the Allies so that she could not challenge British naval supremacy again.

···⟩ Activity

Work in groups of three. Within your group, each person should take on the role of one of the 'Big Three' – Lloyd George, Wilson or Clemenceau.

Your task is to role-play a meeting of the three leaders to discuss what should happen to Germany after the war. Despite differing viewpoints, you have to reach an agreed decision about each of the following issues:

- What should happen to the Kaiser?

- Should Germany be blamed for starting the war?

- Should Germany be made to pay for all the costs of the war?

- What should happen to Germany's armed forces?

- What land, if any, should be taken from Germany?

Report back to the rest of the class on the agreed decisions that you have reached.

THE TERMS OF THE TREATY OF VERSAILLES, 1919

By the terms of the treaty:

Germany lost land

Germany lost about thirteen per cent of her European lands and about ten per cent of her population as a result of the settlement. The lost lands included about 75 per cent of her iron ore. In addition, she lost all of her colonies which were to be handed over to the new League of Nations.

The territorial terms of the Treaty of Versailles, 1919.

The Rhineland was demilitarised

Germany was allowed to keep the Rhineland but all German soldiers and military equipment were banned from the area which was 'demilitarised'. Allied troops would occupy part of the area.

When the terms of the Treaty of Versailles became public, many people pointed out that when Germany signed the Treaty of Brest-Litovsk with Russia in March 1918 (see page 60), the Germans took far more territory and economic resources from Russia than the Allies took from Germany in 1919. In comparison with the Treaty of Brest-Litovsk, Germany was treated lightly.

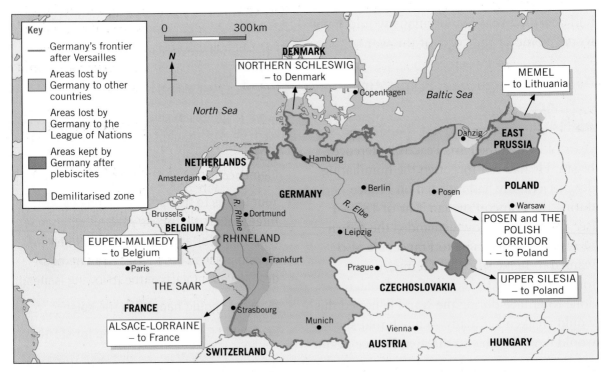

···> Activity

Copy the table below.

Using the map above to help you, explain why each area of land shown on the map was taken from Germany in 1919. The first explanation has been done for you.

Land taken from Germany	Reason for this decision
Alsace and Lorraine were returned to France.	Germany had taken them from France in 1871.

Germany was disarmed

The German army was reduced to 100,000 men and conscription was banned. The navy was reduced to six battleships. Germany was not allowed to keep any submarines and the German air force was disbanded.

None of the victorious countries disarmed at the end of the First World War.

The *Anschluss* was forbidden

By the terms of the treaty, Germany and Austria were forbidden to unite to form one country.

The War Guilt Clause

Article 231 of the Treaty of Versailles blamed Germany and her allies for starting the First World War (see Source B). This part of the treaty is known as the War Guilt Clause.

Source B

Germany accepts the responsibility of Germany and her allies for causing all the loss and damage to which the Allied governments have been subjected as a consequence of the war imposed upon them by the aggression of Germany and her allies.

Article 231 of the Treaty of Versailles, 1919.

Reparations

Because Germany had been blamed for starting the war, she was forced to pay huge sums of money to the Allies (reparations) by Article 232 of the treaty.

Source C

Germany undertakes that she will make compensation for all damage done to the civilian population of the Allied powers and to their property.

Article 232 of the Treaty of Versailles, 1919.

The actual amount of compensation was not fixed until 1921, when it was decided that Germany should pay £6600 million to the Allies. Although this was about half of what the French demanded, it was almost impossible to imagine how Germany could repay this amount of money.

1 Were the military terms of the treaty unfair to Germany?

2 Why was the *Anschluss* forbidden by the Treaty of Versailles?

3 Why is Article 231 of the treaty known as the War Guilt Clause?

4 Were the Allies justified in forcing Germany to sign Articles 231 and 232 of the Treaty of Versailles?

... IN CONCLUSION

- The process of peacemaking in 1919 was flawed.
- The leaders of Britain, France and the USA, the 'Big Three', had very different aims for the peace settlement.
- The Treaty of Versailles was a dictated peace.
- Germany lost land and was disarmed. Germany also had to accept the War Guilt Clause and pay reparations to the Allies.
- Many Germans were angry and ashamed of the Treaty of Versailles.

PRACTISE YOUR ENQUIRY SKILLS

Source D

> Despite the terms of the Treaty of Versailles, Germany retained a strong economic, industrial and territorial position at the heart of Europe, with a vigorous and expanding population of 66 million. The peace settlement left Germany in a potentially dominant position in Europe, wounded but not seriously hurt.

Ruth Henig, a modern historian, writing in 2002.

1   Discuss Ruth Henig's opinion (Source D) of the territorial terms of the Treaty of Versailles.

Source E

> VENGEANCE! GERMAN NATION!
>
> Today in the Hall of Mirrors a disgraceful Treaty is being signed.
>
> Never forget it!
>
> On the spot where, in the glorious year of 1871, the German Empire in all its glory began, today German honour is dragged to the grave.
>
> Never forget it!
>
> The German people, with unceasing labour, will push forward to reconquer that place among the nations of the world to which they are entitled. There will be vengeance for the shame of 1919.

From a German newspaper, *Deutsche Zeitung*, 28 June 1919.

2   How useful is Source E as evidence of the attitude of the German people towards the Treaty of Versailles?

EXTENDED WRITING PRACTISE

3   'An Unjust Peace.'
     How far do you agree with this verdict on the Treaty of Versailles?
     To answer this question, you should write a short essay of several paragraphs.
     Remember to include an introduction to your essay and a conclusion.

4   Imagine that it is 1919 and you are a German who has just read the article in the *Deutsche Zeitung* (Source E).
     Write a letter to the editor of the newspaper, expressing your views of the Treaty of Versailles.
     ■   Try to make your letter as convincing as possible.
     ■   Use your knowledge of the terms of the Treaty to justify your point of view.

THE SEARCH FOR PEACE: THE LEAGUE OF NATIONS, 1919–28

How successful was the League of Nations in the 1920s?

What's it all about?

The League of Nations was established to prevent war in the future. Although many countries joined the League, the USA was never a member. There were weaknesses in the League's organisation and it suffered setbacks in the 1920s. Nevertheless, during the 1920s, the League settled some international disputes and dealt successfully with social and humanitarian issues.

THE BIRTH OF THE LEAGUE OF NATIONS

The last of President Wilson's Fourteen Points (see pages 84–5) stated that an international peacekeeping organisation, the League of Nations, should be established to solve disputes between nations in the future.

The aims and organisation of the League were agreed at the Paris Peace Conference and written down in the League Covenant. This consisted of 26 articles which all members had to accept. At the time, many people believed that the League of Nations would guarantee peace and security throughout the world.

The League met for the first time in 1920. It had its headquarters in Geneva, because Switzerland was a neutral country. Talented people from all over the world set to work to try to put the League's aims into practice. Within five years, there were 55 member states.

What were the main aims of the League?

Article 10 of the Covenant committed all members of the League to the idea of 'collective security'. Each member promised to respect the independence of other members, and to take whatever action the League thought necessary to protect a member that was threatened by another state.

Source A

The members of the League undertake to respect and preserve against external aggression the territorial integrity and existing political independence of all members of the League. In the case of any such aggression or in case of any threat or danger of such aggression, the Council shall advise upon the means by which this obligation shall be fulfilled.

Article 10 of the League Covenant.

Member states also agreed that the League should:

- settle disputes between countries
- oversee international disarmament
- supervise the administration of Germany's former colonies and the Turkish Empire in the Middle East
- promote international cooperation throughout the world.

Glossary

unanimous: every person in agreement.

veto: reject.

sanction: a military or economic penalty.

mandate: the power given to a member state by the League of Nations to govern a region elsewhere.

---

1   Explain what is meant by 'collective security'.

2   Explain how the League aimed to promote world peace.

How was the League organised?

The Assemby

- Met once a year.
- Every member had one vote.
- All decisions had to be **unanimous**.
- Voted for new League members.
- Voted on the budget of the League.
- Voted for non-permanent members of the Council.

The Council

- Met three times a year and eight in emergencies.
- Consisted of permanent and non-permanent members.
- At first, permanent members were Britain, France, Japan and Italy. In 1926, Germany became a permanent member.
- All permanent members could **veto** decisions.
- The Council tried to resolve international disputes.
- If its decisions were not accepted, it could impose **sanctions**.

The Permanent Secretariat

The International Civil Service:
- kept records of meetings
- prepared reports.

The Permanent Court of International Justice

- Could advise the Council and Assembly.
- Could give decisions on border disputes.
- Did *not* have the power to make sure its rulings were obeyed.

International Labour Organisation

Helped improve working conditions.

Mandates Commission

Made sure that the former Empires of Germany and Turkey were well run.

Health Commission

- Spread knowledge of diseases.
- Attempted to deal with dangerous diseases.

Slavery Commission

- Worked to abolish slavery throughout the world.

Refugee Commission

- Helped refugees and prisoners of war.

The organisation of the League of Nations.

What happened if there was an international dispute?

If a dispute was referred to the League of Nations, it would normally be discussed in the Council and, in due course, the Council would issue a report, making recommendations.

If these recommendations were ignored, and the situation deteriorated, the Council could impose sanctions on the country that was at fault. This meant that they could ask other member states to stop trading with the offending country.

If the use of sanctions failed, the Council could ask League members to provide troops for military action. However, the League did not have its own army, and member states were not required to provide soldiers to enforce League policies, so in practice it was hard to enforce decisions. This meant that, in difficult situations, the League could find itself without any effective power.

> 1   Describe the functions of the Assembly, the Council and the Permanent Secretariat. Use the diagram on page 90 to help you.
>
> 2   Describe some of the weaknesses in the organisation of the League.

WHAT WERE THE WEAKNESSES OF THE LEAGUE OF NATIONS?

- The League did not include all nations as members.
- For much of the 1920s, Britain and France dominated the League; neither nation agreed about what the League should try to achieve.
- One of the League's main aims was to oversee disarmament but it failed in this respect.
- The League failed in its aim to resolve international disputes peacefully.

Why did the League not include all nations as members?

Although Germany was still a powerful country, at first she was not allowed to join the League. By 1926, international relations had improved and Germany was given a permanent seat on the Council. However, when Hitler came to power in 1933, Germany withdrew from the League.

Communist Russia (the Soviet Union) was not a member of the League until 1934. This meant that another very powerful country was not a part of the League throughout the 1920s.

Most importantly, the USA never joined the League. Although President Wilson wanted the USA to become a member, the US Senate refused to commit the USA to joining the League. Many Americans believed that League membership would mean further involvement in international affairs, and the USA preferred to follow a foreign policy of isolation and concentrate instead on its own domestic affairs. This meant that the world's greatest power was not a member of the League of Nations.

Source B

THE GAP IN THE BRIDGE.

A *Punch* cartoon of 1920, 'The Gap in the Bridge'. The man in the cartoon is Uncle Sam, representing the USA.

Britain and France dominated the League for much of the 1920s

Because the USA did not join the League of Nations, Britain and France dominated the Council during the 1920s. This meant that some people viewed the League as an organisation for Germany's former enemies, and also believed it had been established to enforce the Treaty of Versailles. The French wanted to increase the power of the League so that it could protect France if Germany were to attack, while Britain was determined to avoid too much involvement in disputes outside Europe. As a result, France and Britain did not always work together in the League.

Source C

TOWSER'LL SEE HE STAYS PUT.
—Peace in the Newark News.

A cartoon from the *Newark News*, 1919 – 'Towser'll see he stays put.'

The failure to disarm

Source D

The members of the League recognise that the maintenance of peace requires the reduction of national armaments to the lowest point consistent with national safety. The Council, taking account of the geographical situation and circumstances of each state, shall formulate plans for such reduction for the consideration and action of the several governments.

Article 8 of the League Covenant.

The League's attempts to tackle the issue of disarmament did not make much progress. Despite the League's commitment, the French were concerned that if they reduced the size of their army, Germany might be able to attack them again. The French claimed that they needed a large, well-equipped army to guarantee their national safety.

In 1926, the League set up a Preparatory Commission to try to find a way of introducing disarmament. This Commission spent several years discussing the problems associated with disarmament, and it was not until 1932 that the League's Disarmament Conference took place. However, within months of the start of the conference, Hitler came to power in Germany. Hitler was committed to rearming Germany, and not disarmament, so the conference stood little chance of success.

During the 1930s, all countries increased their spending on armaments; the hopes for disarmament were ended.

The League could not always resolve disputes

From the creation of the League of Nations, there were disputes that it did not manage to resolve.

In 1920, the Poles seized the town of Vilnius in Lithuania. The League protested but the Poles refused to withdraw. France did not want to intervene any further because it viewed Poland as a possible ally against Germany; Britain was not prepared to act without the support of France. As a result, the Poles kept Vilnius. It was already clear that the League's powers were limited.

In the 1930s, the League proved powerless in the face of aggression by major powers, such as Japan and Italy.

1   How important was US isolation as a cause of weakness in the League of Nations?

2   Why did it prove so difficult to achieve disarmament?

3   Explain why the League was unable to solve the dispute over Vilnius.

WHAT WERE THE SUCCESSES OF THE LEAGUE OF NATIONS?

Because the League failed to prevent the outbreak of the Second World War in 1939, it is easy to overlook the fact that the League was reasonably successful during the 1920s.

The League was popular with many people

Many people were enthusiastic supporters of the League and believed that it could secure international peace.

The League did settle some disputes

Despite its failure over Vilnius in 1920, the League settled several disputes successfully. According to the Treaty of Versailles, part of Silesia was to belong to Germany and part to Poland. The League organised a **plebiscite** so that the Silesians could vote for which country they wanted to join. The League then divided Silesia in accordance with local people's wishes, and both Poland and Germany accepted the decision.

Promoting international cooperation

Some of the League's most important work was done by the commissions and committees it established to help fight poverty, disease and injustice throughout the world. Although the USA was not a member of the League, the US government cooperated with League members in this work.

■ More than 400,000 prisoners of war were helped to return home after the First World War.

■ By 1920, there were over 1.5 million refugees in Europe. Many were given food, shelter and identity papers which helped them find somewhere to settle permanently.

■ The International Health Organisation worked to improve knowledge of killer diseases such as malaria and sleeping sickness.

■ The League Committees investigated the problems of prostitution, slavery, forced labour and international trade in illegal drugs. As a result of the League's efforts, in 1927, about 200,000 British-owned slaves were freed in Sierra Leone.

■ The International Labour Organisation campaigned for improved working conditions and drew up an international agreement regulating the hours children could work.

Optimism in the 1920s

After the First World War, huge numbers of people throughout the world rejected war as a means of solving international problems. It was an age of widespread **pacifism**, with people determined to make sure that the Great War had indeed been 'the war to end all wars'.

Source E

It is for humanity to choose now which road it wants to take. Will it follow the flag of the old order or the standard of the League of Nations? Under one, the complete breakdown of civilisation and the self-extermination of humankind are only a matter of time; the other leads to unexplored fields of human cooperation and creative labour.

From an article written about the League in 1920.

Glossary

plebiscite: when local people vote on a particular matter.

pacifism: the rejection of all violence and war.

The Locarno Treaties

This worldwide mood led to the signing of various treaties designed to guarantee peace. In 1925, seven European countries, including Britain, France and Germany, signed the Locarno Treaties. As part of these treaties, Germany and France agreed to settle any future disputes through the League of Nations. As a result of these treaties, international relations improved and, the following year, Germany joined the League.

The Kellogg-Briand Pact

In 1928, another peace agreement, known as the Kellogg-Briand Pact, was signed. (This was named after the US secretary of state, Frank Kellogg, and the French foreign minister, Aristide Briand, who drew up the agreement). The Kellogg-Briand Pact seemed particularly significant because the USA was involved. All of the signatories agreed to seek peaceful solutions to disputes, although they recognised that armed forces were necessary for self-defence. Within a few years, 46 countries had signed up to the terms of the Kellogg-Briand Pact.

By 1928, it seemed for a moment as if international cooperation was about to replace international conflict. However, over the next decade there was an increase in foreign aggression and disputes, culminating in the outbreak of the Second World War in 1939. Events during the 1930s thus proved how wrong the belief in international cooperation had been.

···⟩ Activity

1 Draw up a balance sheet showing League strengths and weaknesses in the 1920s.

League strengths in the 1920s	League weaknesses in the 1920s

2 What conclusions can you draw about the League of Nations during the 1920s?

... IN CONCLUSION

- ···⟩ ■ The League of Nations was set up after the First World War to prevent further wars and to promote international cooperation.
- ■ The League was based on a belief in 'collective security'.
- ■ The organisation of the League made it difficult for it to be effective.
- ■ The League suffered from weaknesses from the start, including the USA's refusal to join.
- ■ The League did have some success in the 1920s, especially in tackling social and humanitarian issues.

PRACTISE YOUR ENQUIRY SKILLS

1   What was the attitude of the author of Source E (page 93) towards the League of Nations?

2   How fully do Sources B (page 91) and C (page 92) illustrate the weaknesses of the League of Nations during the 1920s?

INDEX

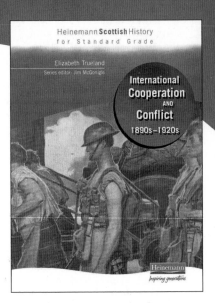